THE PERFECT COUNTRY COTTAGE

BILL LAWS

ABBEVILLE PRESS PUBLISHERS

New York *London* *Paris*

To Abby

Project Editor JOANNA BRADSHAW
Art Editor MERYL LLOYD
Picture Research ABIGAIL AHERN
Production Controller JULIA GOLDING

First American Edition

Published by Abbeville Press.

Printed and bound in China.

ISBN 1-55859-784-0

CONTENTS

A SIMPLE FORM OF LIVING

What is a perfect cottage? And how best can a traditional cottage feel be imparted to a not-so-perfect old building? In the following chapters we explore the origins and sheer variety of the simple country home, from Cornwall to Connecticut, Greece to Grenoble, and offer practical suggestions on how to recreate a country atmosphere in a house that is at home with its local landscape.

More often than not, the exterior of a cottage will offer a few visual clues as to what kind of interior treatment it should be given. For instance, the kitchen of a simple flint cottage with small windows would not benefit from the addition of gleaming stainless steel fitted units – the clash of materials would be too much. Likewise, a light and airy barn conversion would look stark and uninviting if filled with small, low pieces of furniture that did not capitalize on its inherently tall ceilings. The overriding consideration when furnishing a traditional vernacular home should always be to remain faithful to the original structure by making a warm, comfortable interior that does not destroy the original character of the building.

LOCAL DISTINCTIVENESS

This Irish longhouse in County Galway with its stubby chimney, slurried slate roof and bright whitewashed face makes a distinctive contribution to the look of the surrounding landscape.

PERFECT COTTAGES

The concept of the perfect country cottage is one of infinite variety and style. The cottage – a small house which fits harmoniously into its rural setting and whose unselfconscious interior is cosy and welcoming – may be a limestone worker's dwelling in the Cotswolds, a timber-framed house in New England or a tiny stone and thatch shelter in Ireland. Traditionally, these homes were built by local builders using indigenous materials to blend effortlessly into the surrounding natural landscape.

To our modern eyes, the most evocative and atmospheric country homes are those which have retained their original character while having been sympathetically restored using salvaged or carefully reproduced elements such as fireplaces, beams, exposed brick walls, doors, windows and shutters.

From the time when people first settled the land to the contemporary urban longing for an uncomplicated country existence, the unpretentious rural dwelling has retained firm favour in the popular imagination.

STYLE VARIETY

The hard lines of Brittany's indigenous granite are softened on this cottage (above) by the flow of the reed thatch roof which sits above the small dormer window. Brick and timber are the basic materials for this Shaker-style home in the United States (right). Locally-made brick forms the fireproof hearth and chimney indoors, while outdoors, clapboard is used to face and protect the building's façade.

EXTERIORS

Different people have different ideas about what constitutes the perfect country cottage. For a modern family of Boston back-to-the-landers perfection could mean an ecologically sound timber-framed cabin standing on fertile soil and close, but not too close, to the village school and grocery store. Their counterparts in a Stockholm suburb might prefer a user-friendly small house with a distinctly country feel and all the amenities of modern life. In Milan, meanwhile, the idyllic retreat for city-weary people might be a winter chalet high up on an isolated mountain pass.

The common thread running through these lives is the desire to live in simple, country-style surroundings, in harmony with the rural environment. This universal desire knows no geographical boundaries and has given us a rich variety of vernacular building styles.

Take the reed-thatched and whitewashed Camargue cabane and the snow white clapboard of a small Massachusetts farmhouse. Both employ the three basic materials common to all cottage building – timber, earth and stone – yet the two buildings are as far apart in looks as they are in distance. Designs vary from country to country, region to region, even from village to village. Among the apple orchards and cattle pastures of French Normandy one village is dominated by low, long houses with a crest of lilies on their thatched ridges; in the next village sturdy limestone houses with dark slate roofs predominate because of the local

abundance of these materials. Before cheap, mass produced materials became widely available, each parish built its homes from whatever lay close to hand. Function rather than fashion ruled the vernacular look.

But the see-saw world of style and design has regularly paid homage to the small country dwelling. Before losing her head on Doctor Guillotin's machine, the 17th-century French queen Marie Antoinette eschewed the glitz of Versailles Palace life for the pseudo-country style of Le Hameau. Across the channel in England, William Morris' contempt for conspicuous consumption and opulent artificiality brought about the Arts and Crafts movement, and a renewed appreciation of hand-crafted furniture and fittings.

ATTENTION TO DETAIL

The softwoods of Eastern Europe can be cut and carved into elaborate decorative forms as on this building in Czechoslovakia (above). In Normandy, by contrast, the timber frame of this vernacular farmhouse creates its own decorative pattern (left).

At the end of the twentieth century, individual craftspeople are once more in demand, among them woodturners, carpenters and stonemasons. At the same time, many exterior vernacular features such as half-timbering, dormer windows, half-hipped roofs, country kitchens and ledge-and-brace doors have become standard elements in the design of countless housing estates. The cottage tradition lives on.

COTTAGES AND THE LANDSCAPE

Why does a Cumbrian cottage with its black stone and green slate roof differ so dramatically from a simple Mediterranean house with walls of whitewashed rubble and a roof of Roman tiles? The answer is the vernacular building tradition. Vernacular is the Latin word for a slave born in his master's house and thus a native. Vernacular buildings are those that are native to their own province.

Such folk buildings were among the earliest forms of architecture and it is the tried and tested methods of vernacular building design that have endured long enough to inform the design process of many a modern skyscraper. But a legacy of traditional buildings survives around the world: red, Roman-tiled farmhouses in southern France; reed and timber marshland huts in Italy's Caserta region and settlers' timber cottages on the east coast of America.

These buildings mirror the underlying groundstones, slipping inconspicuously into the surrounding countryside and colouring our judgement about what looks right and proper in the countryside. As William Wordsworth put it, they 'may rather be said to have grown than to have been erected – to have risen by an instinct of their own, out of the native rock – so little is there in them of formality, such is their wildness and beauty.'

Wordsworth was referring to his native Cumbrian cot, sheltering in the lea of some craggy fell, its rough stone walls bright with whitewash, and its two tubby chimneys poking out from a roof of Westmoreland slate. He might have said the same thing about a Finnish log cabin, sheathed in weathered, vertical boards, its open-air gallery looking out across a vast area of birchwood scrub. The two scenes are as purposeful as they are picturesque, for each building evolved to make the best use of local climate and topography.

VERNACULAR RESPONSE

In the English lakelands (right), rugged Cumbrian stone is used to build farms and cottages. A French farmhouse in the Vallée du Var (top left) boasts a roof of Roman tiles, or tuiles á canal. *Where local stone was poor, tin and timber were called into service (centre left). A neat cabin on the island of Grenada (bottom left) displays a colourful exterior.*

LOCAL MATERIALS

BUILT BY HAND

A growing awareness of vernacular furnishings, fixtures and features such as those at Kennixton (above right), an early seventeenth-century farmhouse rebuilt at the Welsh Folk Museum in South Wales, has led to a growing interest in their care and preservation.

Vernacular buildings were traditionally constructed as a direct response to regional climate and conditions, without the aid of architects. These decorated timber homes beside a Romanian road (below right) reflect local decorative building traditions and a sensitive use of colour.

MATERIAL VALUE

The arrival of cheap, mass-produced building materials finally brought the vernacular tradition, typified by the beautiful beehived roofs on this Dordogne farmhouse (above left), to a close.

New ideas and new materials such as the gable end hearths and chimney pots on this Hebridean croft (below left) gradually filtered through to remote regions.

Increasingly, homes like these are being discreetly brought up to date indoors despite the conservation of practical exterior features such as the thatch roof.

RESTORING ORIGINAL FEATURES

- *Tracing the history of your home can be an absorbing task. Try to establish the original layout of the cottage. Built-up doorways or the remains of an old arch in a wall are useful clues, while a stone lower floor with a half-timbered upper floor suggests that the second storey was a later addition to the building.*

- *Most small country houses functioned as both home and workplace. The original layout will often reveal its former use: an open-plan upper floor lit by unusually large windows could indicate a cottage weaving gallery; a slab-floored cellar with a drain down the centre may be the remains of a wine or beer store from a former inn.*

- *Look at the exterior materials; handmade bricks are irregular in both shape and colour, while Roman bricks, still in use today, are twice the length and half the thickness of a conventional brick. Check whether the outside facing material of brick, boarding or render conceals older material.*

- *Although most roofs will have been stripped and replaced every century, they are a useful key to the past. Explore the roof space where former timbers will be retained; smoke blackened timbers indicate an old hall house, once open up to the roof.*

- *Documentary evidence on small, rural homes is often rudimentary but parish records, early maps and estate journals are good starting places. If your home was once a working building like a mill, farmhouse, café or smithy, there is a better chance of it having been recorded somewhere.*

- *Datestones and commemorative inscriptions are helpful although they were often inscribed to celebrate a rebuilding rather than the founding of the cottage. Tracing back the original cottage name can also provide pertinent clues as to its origins.*

CLUES TO THE PAST

The cart doors, stone slate roof and old-fashioned chimney, built before chimney pots came into fashion, all provide clues to the age of this cottage (opposite top).

Never judge a house by its roof – the steep pitch of the clay tile roof on this former farmhouse in the Massif Central region of France suggests an original covering of thatch (left).

A guide to the original purpose of a country home often lies in specialist outbuildings such as this circular hop kiln and adjoining cooling house (opposite bottom) in Kent, England.

Chapter One

FIRST IMPRESSIONS

Glimpsing a country cottage for the first time can be a joyous experience. Greeted by graceful, ancient roses ranged round a snug porch, wisteria draped sineously from a gabled portico, or walls washed in warm terracotta, who would not be completely consumed by a delightful sense of expectation?

Country cottages blend into the landscape without being inconspicuous, they rise proudly from the earth which, more often than not, fashioned their framework and shaped their exterior. Such traditional buildings have often stood their ground unchanged for centuries, having become part and parcel of the local culture.

Despite apparent similarities, no two cottages are exactly the same. Each has reflected the individuality of its inhabitants for a century or so and a careful appraisal of all its inherent exterior details, whether they be original features or unsuccessful replacements, needs to be carried out before sympathetic restoration work begins.

SHELTERING THATCH

A glorious fusion of wild flowers and herbs provides a rich and colourful welcome at this English country cottage near Sidbury in Dorset. A brick-built extension has been sympathetically grafted on to the older, whitewashed part of the house by carrying the rolling thatch across both roofs.

MAKING AN ENTRANCE

The quiet calm of a cottage approach, with its sea of proud, fragrant hollyhocks and foxgloves, or a façade of brilliant white stone and crisply contrasting black-painted woodwork certainly lends credence to the idea that country living is clean and healthy and good for the soul.

A traditional cottage is usually sited on a weathertight plot to make the best use of all the elements. Hedged against cold winds and open to the sunny south, a kitchen garden was often to be found, set close to the house so as to shorten the regular journeys between the herb bed and the cooking pot, not to mention the frequent journeys between the water supply and the tin bath.

Any path was purely for pedestrians, but for the modern cottage a driveway is just as essential. The appearance of bulldozer tracks through a cottage hedgebank is one of the early warning signs that an old house is about to be brought up to date. The drive which thrusts its way to the cottage door like a miniature motorway is an ominous sign: is the old house being bullied unceremoniously into the twentieth century? Or will the character of the building and its furnishings be tastefully retained? The entranceway to a country cottage and the first impressions it bestows on a visitor is as important to its overall character as is a careful and sensitive choice of furniture and fittings indoors.

WHITEWASHED STONE

A mossy thatch roof (left) butts up to plain stone parapets on this whitewashed cottage. Rainwater gutters were not traditionally applied to thatched houses, so a black tar surround was used to protect the base of the walls from water splashing against them.

WATERPROOF WEATHERBOARD

Yellow flag irises (above) stand sentinel at the gateway leading to a seventeenth-century whipple house near Ipswich, Massachusetts. The original timber for the shingle roof and clapboard will have been obtained from local woodlands.

BEATING A PATH

Before the advent of the automobile, the cottage lay as close to the thoroughfare as a goose to its down. The small country house showed its best profile to the roadside as visitors stepped off the curtilage straight into the front door. It was a necessarily short journey, given that everything from the annual apple crop to the daily bucket of water had to be carried over the threshold. But, as passing traffic began to disrupt this previously peaceful state of affairs, the cottager closed off the front door and ran a path round to the back, making an entranceway at the rear.

Since fruit and flowers grew round the back, the idea of being led up these garden paths was more a pleasure than a deceit. River gravel, broken roof slates, stone slabs and brick or pounded dirt were variously employed to pave a winding way through flower borders and herb beds to the back door. On the cottage itself, damp-proof courses were rare and rain-water gutters rudimentary or non-existent; on the earth or cob cottage, a well-tended grit or gravel path was a necessity since the skirting path drained away surface water.

In the timber-rich territories of Scandinavia or among the forests of North America, a plank and pole boardwalk carried the visitor to the cabin doorstep. Not only did the creaking pathway keep the housewife's skirts out of the winter mud, its echoing footfalls also warned her of approaching guests. In southern Europe, a visitor's clogs were more likely to resound against compacted road stone or granite cobbles along paths which led to the terrace or patio, where the al fresco life of the Mediterranean household rumbled amiably along from generation to generation.

GARDEN PATH

A studded oak door in Hartland, Devon (above left) is entirely in keeping with the stone doorway and slate steps, while a timber-clad porch protects a plain ledge-and-brace door (above right).

Framed by tree boughs, this wide brick path meanders gently to the doorstep (right). To create a similar effect, use old, irregular bricks and bed them in sand or earth. They will gradually slip and settle into comfortable undulations.

3100

THROUGH THE GARDEN GATE

- *Break up hard surfaces on a newly restored property with greenery. Trelliswork fixed to freshly painted wall surfaces can be used to train climbers such as wisteria and grapevines. Some vigorous climbers, such as Virginia creeper and Boston ivy, will need to be cut back after their spectacular autumn colours have faded and changed.*

- *Scented climbing roses, jasmine or clematis look stunning and produce a lingering perfume when planted beside a door and trained into a flowering arch.*

- *Take care not to plant shrubs close to rainwater drains or gullies, as plant roots can block drains and cause damp problems.*

- *Use container-grown shrubs and trees as decorative green pillars ranged along a cottage wall, but remember that plants in pots need to be fed and watered.*

- *Try to preserve the essential character of the cottage when adding on porches, garages or other outbuildings.*

- *Choose downwater pipes in neutral colours or tone down plastic piping with dark or grey spray paint. Reroot supply lines away from the best face of the building or have them brought to the house below ground.*

- *Depending on local reception, television aerials can be removed from the chimney and re-sited indoors, in the loft.*
- *Fuel stores such as oil or gas tanks need to be close to the house and accessible for deliveries. Site them as unobtrusively as possible, boxing them in behind wicker hurdles or trelliswork covered with evergreen plants such as philodendrons or ivies.*
- *Avoid planting a privacy screen of evergreen trees which will grow into a light-blocking barrier.*

A FLORAL WELCOME

Original shutters painted powder blue (opposite top), make a delightful contrast to the terracotta walls and generous trailing greenery of this rural home in southern France.

A charming flint cottage (opposite below) nestles behind a tall walkway of traditional garden plants and provides a warm welcome.

A tangled cottage garden brimming with foxgloves and a delightful rambling rose (above right) provides a perfect entrance for this country house.

Dripping with mature wisteria flowers, this half-timbered English house (below right) is engulfed by colour each summer.

PAINTED EXTERIORS

Cottages and country houses have presented a painted face to the world from the earliest of times, partly to make them stand out amongst the greenery of the countryside and partly to weatherproof them from the elements.

Whitewash made with chalk dust, size and milk was the most common treatment, sometimes confined to front walls or doorways alone, but earth-colour washes were common throughout Europe from medieval times. Bright yellows, blues, burnt umbers and ochres were drawn from local materials, and whole villages reflected the colour of their surroundings. In Rustrel in southern France, houses were painted with red pigment from the neighbouring groundstones, while in Saffron Walden in eastern England, homes were coloured using the saffron crocus grown in the region.

White lead paints were popular treatments for window frames, while exposed softwood timbers were picked out in darker blacks and blues, primarily for protection. The habit of painting oak blue, brown or the black so typical of middle England was more decorative than practical, since the natural silver-grey oak would season like iron and outlast its surrounding wattle and daub.

Choosing exterior house colours today is less a question of available colours – the range of external paints and pigments is almost limitless – but more one of available light. The faded pinks and yellow ochres of a Mediterranean fishing village look at home in the crisp, bright winter morning light. But such colours would not travel well to the honey-gold limestone cottages of the French Dordogne or to the English Cotswolds.

Be guided both by the age of your home and by local tradition. In the Labourd region of the Basque country, where threads of red pimentos drying in the sun decorate the house walls, timberwork looks spectacular painted in strident reds and greens against a sparkling whitewash; in western Ireland, the inhabitants are ready to risk a sharp yellow or red ground floor against a white painted upper floor and to paint the doors and windows in cheerfully contrasting lime green.

Experiment with different colours on a tracing of the

cottage drawn from a large-scale photograph. Having made your choice, remember to use permeable paints which will let bare stone or brickwork breathe. Repeating the wall colours on doors, windows and shutters can work well on clapboard buildings, while contrasting tones such as red window and door frames against stone or brick, or black frames against a whitewashed wall, can be effective.

Exterior ornamentation was rarely found on the unfussy exteriors of most country cottages, so care should be taken to preserve unusual features that are still intact, such as datestones, carvings or wall paintings.

MATCHING PAIR

As a general rule, the smaller the window, the older the house. These two windows (far left above) on a cottage built of bare earth and thatched with raw reeds are protected by the deep eaves of the roof.

LEAN-TO LOOK

The convention of building windows into a cottage as the house rose was not followed on log cabins (far left below). Instead window and door openings were sawn through after the walls had been built, hence the asymmetrical appearance of this pair of windows on a log house.

CLASSIC FRANCE

The characteristic Mediterranean window is narrow, deep and sheltered by old wooden shutters. Here (above left) the window surrounds are picked out in pink against the whitewashed walls. A window box filled with petunias completes the scene.

SWISS SGRAFFITI

This window set deep in the wall of a Swiss building in the Eurgadine region (below left) is surrounded by sgraffiti decoration. Features like these, though more common in central and highland Europe, are rare, so they should be preserved and maintained.

FRAMING THE VIEW

Until the nineteenth century, the durable wooden shutter was once the only answer to letting in the best, and keeping out the worst, of the weather. The clatter of little timber doors being opened or closed has echoed across the continents at sunrise and sunset ever since.

Early shutters comprised freestanding wooden frames which were lifted into place at sunset. But by the eighteenth century they were hinged on metal pins that had been driven into the wall, fitted with louvred sections to circulate fresh air or, a favourite custom in Alpine regions, pierced with a decorative eye-hole, shaped like the native fir tree.

And by the nineteenth century, most shutters closed against glazed windows. Initially glass was too expensive for the average cottager; those who could afford window panes across their 'windholes' regarded them as furniture and floorboards and took all with them when they moved. Although the Romans had manufactured glass, the conventional cottage window held the elements at bay with anything but glass: slivers of pale, thin horn; alabaster; oiled paper; even the placenta of cattle or horses was used instead.

When affordable glass arrived on the market, it was cut into small diamond shapes then set in lead, like many church windows. Cheaper sheet glass lead to the Dutch-designed sliding sash windows spreading across Europe in the early nineteenth century, while the horizontal sliding sash appeared on low-browed cottages that featured two tiny windows tucked under the eaves. A century later, cast-iron casements were popular until they too were replaced by modern timber casements.

Redundant hop kilns, old boathouses, workshops, cow sheds and hay barns have all been converted into cottages and many have distinctive windows which tell something of their past. Typical examples are pitching eyes set in the gable wall of a building and used to pitchfork winter supplies of hay into the old barn, or small oval or semi-circular openings set under the eaves to circulate fresh air around the loft.

Cottage windows and other features like them are the eyes of the house. Replace them with wide expanses of toughened glass, mock-Georgian units or aluminium frames and it has the same visual impact as removing the back lawn and relaying plastic grass. However, by returning windows to their original style, by having them specially made and by using sympathetic window treatments on the inside, you can restore rather than ruin a traditional cottage.

As a rough guide, the older the house, the smaller the window and diminutive windows restrict both the light and the view. The conventional four-paned window can be replaced with a deeper nine- or twelve-paned frame and the heat loss of the increased area reduced by the addition of secondary glazing or indoor shutters.

Old windows are often made of a superior hardwood and can be given a new lease of life by replacing rotten sections, usually the sill, and painting the repair. New wooden casements must be painted or, to reduce maintenance, treated with a stain. Pick out frames and sills in white or pale colours – dark colours tend to demote and camouflage the windows, especially against shadowy stone buildings – and use a pale colour inside to reflect more light into the rooms. French windows which open out onto a patio or garden add a sense of space to a room and allow light to flood in. In warmer weather they can be left open during the day to let fresh air circulate through the room. On the inside, hang generous fabric curtains or old lace, rather than venetian blinds, which would look too harsh.

VERNACULAR SIMPLICITY

This small but beautiful window is set into a limewashed wall which nestles under a wooden shingle roof. Metal brackets have been used to reinforce the opening and extend the life of the old casement.

SHUTTERS

- *Shutters are an important vernacular detail, exhibiting both the aesthetic and practical nature of traditional building techniques.*
- *The metal hooks from which shutters hang are weak points in the design and will need replacing from time to time.*
- *Recycle old metalwork handles, hooks and bars which are often cast in unusual designs such as a clenched fist or open hand. Clean the metal with a sand blaster or wire brush and paint it with a protective coat of metal paint.*
- *Timber shutters will need to be repainted from time to time. Rub down the old paint, clean the wood with white spirit and repaint. Modern stains and microporous paints which allow the wood to breathe are preferable on new softwoods.*
- *Using louvred external shutters as ornamentation on Northern cottages can look out of place. They are better sited indoors in cold climates.*

OPEN HOUSE

This wall clock and shutters (above left), are typical of a high Alpine village.

The louvred and panelled shutters on these cottage walls (far left below, left, and right) filter light and fresh air into the interior.

DOORS

The door is the key exterior element of any house. It is the first feature people notice and, whether they strike the grinning devil doorknocker or lift the latch, the door is the first device they use, so first impressions count.

During the eighteenth century, doors were still so small that they would barely reach above the shoulders of a modern-day teenager. Small but heavy, these wooden doors were hung on strap hinges from proper door frames, fitted with ornamental metal latches and, after the invention of the concealed mortice lock, very occasionally armed with a lock. Like the modern burglar alarm, the presence of a prominent keyhole suggested there might be something worth stealing in the cottage. There rarely was, and until the late nineteenth century locks were only significant as a sign of social status rather than as security devices.

Mass-produced panelled doors eventually came into general use in the nineteenth century, when the solid ledge-and-brace door was relegated to the woodshed or cut down to fit a bedroom. A similar fate befell both the door divided vertically down the middle and the useful heck-door or stable door, divided horizontally and used to let light and air into the kitchen, while keeping stray hens and the farmhouse dog out. Both types are now in regular use again in many renovated country cottages.

External doors these days should be made of hardwood and furnished with door handles and knockers of painted cast iron rather than brass or aluminium. In some cases, a repaired door is superior to a brand new door, which is likely to be flimsily made and expensive, or both. The first signs of wear on an old door appear around the bottom weather-board and on the lower panels. They can be repaired easily by jointing-in new sections.

Traditionally, it was common practice throughout rural Europe to pick out the doorframe in whitewash, a technique which served the practical purpose of guiding the small-holders back to their thresholds on dark, moonless nights. Where the door and window frames are white, the door itself can take a contrastingly bright colour.

OGEE ARCH

Ornamentation on old country cottages was often confined to a simple arched doorway (opposite left). Four quarter lights have been added to the door to lighten the hallway beyond.

GREY SLATE FACE

The plain panelled door on this Welsh cottage (opposite right) is surrounded by a sea of slate. Slates or tiles form a weatherproof finish to west-facing walls.

CELTIC CUSTOMS

The habit of leaving the granite doorway free of whitewash was common all along the western seaboard of Europe and focused attention on the central painted front door (right).

PORCHES AND VERANDAS

The Southern terrace, patio or veranda is as necessary to the well-being of a householder as the shaded porch is to those in the North. Verandas were traditionally adopted by British colonials to make the most of the outdoors without having to face glaring sunlight or suffer heatstroke. American settlers also found them useful, since the addition of a generous timber deck could double the living space of a classic country cottage. Unlike the Spanish, who preferred the Moorish privacy of an inner courtyard, the American settlers, like their Scandinavian forefathers, liked to sit and watch the world go by from their front porches.

The veranda has always been an intrinsic part of the house, sheltered by a shingle roof and sometimes enclosed by ivy-clad latticework. But the Northern porch was often an afterthought. Even in the bleakest, most windswept regions of western England, outside porches did not appear until the end of the sixteenth century.

On larger cottages and farmhouses, the porch might be a two-storey edifice, the upper storey incorporating a cold larder or spare bed chamber, lit by an oriel window. On smaller, single-storey cottages such as the granite Devon longhouse, the porch was built as broad as an ox, with flanking walls deep enough to deflect side winds. Often a stone or slate bench was inserted into the east wall to catch the late-day sun.

Midway between north and south, in the predictably

damper climates of the west coasts of France, Britain and Ireland, a simpler solution was the door hood, made from thatch and timber or a creeper-laden trellis beneath a lead or slate hood. In Brittany, a favourite late nineteenth-century design was a door hood of glass and wrought-iron, also adopted to shelter the family headstone in the local village graveyard.

These days, outdoors leads indoors through a hall. The 'hall' in medieval times was the main room of a building where the inhabitants lived, ate and slept while a 'porch' was an inner, draught-proof room between the door and the hall. In the traditional longhouse design, cattle and kin were separated from each other by a cross passage running from the front to the back doors. Eventually the passage was closed off to create a storage space for the clutter of waterproofs and galoshes.

SHADE AND SHELTER

A wide and weathertight timber deck beneath an extension to a house roof provides extra living and storage space (opposite).
Trailing wisteria and a simple porch hood screen the face of this brick and flint cottage (top left).
The materials used to add a broad porch to this half-timbered house faithfully follow the older timber framing with brick infill (above left).
The L-shaped corner of this American clapboard house is an ideal location for an open veranda, providing a place to sit, eat and relax (above).

HALLWAYS

A north- or west-facing hall will let in the weather and let out the heat every time the door is opened, while the door leading to a south-facing hall will tend to be left open on sunny days. Since all house traffic will constantly pass through it, the cottage hall needs to be light, hardwearing and uncluttered.

Where space is at a premium, and the hall has been built merely as a convention to some forgotten fashion, the room can be removed altogether. In northern areas a weathertight porch would suffice, while in warm southern regions an open trellised porch would work well.

Natural daylight is the ideal lighting for a hall. In the absence of a window, consider using a half-glazed door, veiled with a thin curtain for privacy. Alternatively, build a fanlight above the door.

Hardwearing floors, such as tiles, stone flags or wooden boards are preferable to carpeting since, in the winter months, much of the outside will inevitably find its way inside.

Hall walls tend to suffer more than their fair share of scuff marks. Washable wallpapers provide some protection, but opt for light colours to avoid creating a gloomy entrance.

WELCOME HOME

The glimpse of an upstairs room, a view of the Tuscan hills and a welcoming tray of fruit lend this farmhouse a warm and hospitable feel (opposite).

The pale colours in this Umbrian farmhouse hall (left) have been carried up across the ceiling to reflect the natural daylight flooding in from a central window. Simple ornaments, a delightful small table and chair and an enchanting frieze make the room both useful and welcoming.

Simple flagstones, limewashed walls and bare ceiling timbers act as a backcloth to old, flamboyantly painted, vertically divided doors set deep in the wall (above).

HALL FURNITURE

The transition area from outdoors to indoors should be made warm and welcoming: crossing the threshold though the stable-type door onto the broad-timbered floor of this Polish house (right), with its bright rag throws and warm red paintwork, provides an agreeable encounter.

A pleasantly cool reception awaits the visitor to this Greek cottage (far left above). The low doorway is a familiar feature in traditional country homes, built in the days when the average height of the occupants would have been much lower than today.

A Scandinavian hall provides decoration in the form of painted geometric shapes on the walls and swirling designs on the floor (above left).

White entranceways like these (far left below) which reflect the maximum amount of light into what would otherwise be a dim and gloomy hall passage, work well in any climate. Provide a Shaker pegrail and some interesting hangers, and you can create an inviting hallway in the most spartan of country houses.

There is a minimum of fuss or furniture to meet the visitor in this tiled Greek entrance hall (below left). Just a cane-backed rocking chair, an ornamental pot and a plain back door framed by bare granite adorn the space.

FLOORS

A century ago the most likely surface to meet the feet of the cottage visitor was either a highly polished, shiny floor of pounded earth or bleached wooden floorboards. Earth was turned to a tough, resilient finish by mixing the local soil, preferably a good clay, with anything from skimmed milk to bull's blood. The surface was then beaten smooth with wooden boards or, in Ireland at least, by inviting the neighbours in for a floor-flattening dance. Earth floors were inclined to be dusty and laid with rushes, or in Norway, strewn with juniper twigs and dampened with water. Occasionally the earth floor was reinforced by setting animal bones in the earth to form a curious, but hardwearing cobbled finish.

Sound timber floors were relatively rare in the humble cottage before the nineteenth century, when protecting them against the ravages of time, and pressure from hob-nailed boots, was a perennial problem.

In Norway, the boards were scrubbed with wet sand until they took on the colour of sea-bleached flotsam. An easier way to achieve the same effect is to knock in the nail heads, machine-sand the boards and, after a thorough cleaning with white spirit, bleach and wax the wood. In America, people were more inclined to give the boards a fresh coat of paint, while in England they tended to leave well alone and cover those areas of greatest wear with a floor cloth or rug. To paint floorboards use special floor paints, perhaps stencilling a pattern over a light base colour. For polished floors, invest in a floor polisher; after two or three initial applications of wax mixed with linseed oil to feed the clean wood, wax the floors twice a month, depending on wear, and run the polisher over the top. The twentieth-century habit of varnishing the wood is never very successful: in high-wear areas such as halls, varnish tends to chip or wear away.

If an original hall floor is missing, stone flags or terracotta tiles make hardwearing and sensible flooring solutions. The underlying subsoil must be excavated, laid with a damp-proof membrane and a concrete sub-surface and the finished floor surface laid on top. Easy to wipe clean and maintenance-free, such a finished floor is infinitely preferable to fitted carpets, and can be subtly enhanced with a woven rug or runner.

Quarry tiles give a sound and solid finish to a farmhouse floor (above top). At one time different districts produced their own varieties, but the mass-produced Victorian quarry tile swept aside the old village crafts.

Unsympathetic building regulations in some countries insist that ancient pitched stone floors like these (above) should give way to dull concrete. Although difficult to lift and re-lay over a damp-proof membrane, the result more than justifies the painstaking efforts.

Bare boards which have been waxed and lightly polished (right) give a rich finish to the cottage floor. Second-hand boards, denailed and sanded down are preferable and sometimes cheaper than new boards.

Chapter Two

THE HEART OF THE HOME

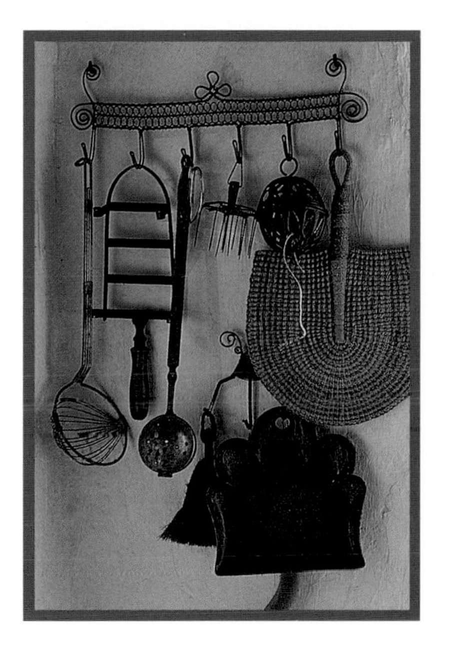

The country kitchen has always been the traditional heart of the home. Centuries ago it was the place where the day's business was discussed over breakfast, where families and their workers shared their meals and where, in the evening, the household gathered by the fireside to take stock of the day's events.

After an uncomfortable period during the 1950s when the kitchen was seen as inferior to the more formal parlour, the classic country kitchen, with its natural materials, spacious seating and informal atmosphere has returned to popular favour with a vengeance. But the kitchen has also had to react to the development of high-tech labour-saving devices such as washing machines and microwave ovens, refrigerators and built-in ovens – all bulky items that have threatened to destroy the character of many older kitchens, turning them in to push-button factories of barefaced steel and clinical plastic. It need not be so. Judicious planning and an inventive use of cupboard space to disguise equipment can mean you are free to recreate an informal atmosphere at the heart of the home.

AQUA WOOD

Imaginatively painted cupboards ranged along one wall make this a practical but comfortable working kitchen that doubles as a family room.

WORKING KITCHENS

The country kitchen is often torn between convenience and convention. The conventional necessities have always been a dependable source of heat, water and storage space, while the conveniences depend upon the technology of the time. The current trend towards fast food and a kitchen cleansed of the smell of cooking has made a god of convenience and a devil of convention. But pristine and clinical fitted units are gradually giving way to individual, painted dressers and shelves; microwaves are being banished to painted cupboards; and ovens, dishwashers and washing machines discreetly tucked away behind wooden doors.

In medieval times, the country kitchen was both workroom and living room, cramped and uncomfortable. Today, as labour-saving devices have taken the physical hardship out of preparing and cooking food, the kitchen has once again become the heart of the country home, a place to meet, eat and live in comfort, with enough space for tables and chairs, as well as a food preparation area.

An original inglenook is an ideal place for the solid-fuel stove which heats the water, the food and the room. Alternatively, a built-in oven and separate hob can be placed between the sink and the refrigerator, with useful work surfaces and cupboards placed in between. To avoid the uniform look of the store-bought kitchen, try customizing wooden units by painting or stencilling them in different colours and replacing door handles. Alternatively, ask a local carpenter to construct the carcassing or cupboard supports to suit your work surfaces and clad them in doors made up

from reclaimed timbers, stained or painted to harmonize with your favourite dresser or fireside settle.

Many cottage kitchens have been enlarged by knocking through a wall to give a generous-sized living area. Where once the larder or dairy stood, utility rooms have been created, allowing the freezer and washing machine, a useful but noisy appliance, to be moved from the kitchen.

The kitchen table, chairs and work surfaces should blend in with the original room. Opt for worktops of natural materials such as slate, tiles, marble or wood, and back them with a frieze of handmade tiles. Position a mismatching row of shelves made from left-over wood above them.

Avoid the regimented style of a completely fitted kitchen and enjoy matching natural textures and materials; an earthenware jug filled with wooden spoons and rolling pins, a bread crock and wicker bowls of fruit and vegetables, old butcher's hooks hung with weathered copper pans and utensils, all sit happily in a country kitchen. Store food mixers and liquidizers in an old pie cupboard or on the lower shelves of the dresser, and the result will be a more harmonious working atmosphere.

HEARTH AND HOME

A traditional cooking fire with its fire bricks and plaster chimney hood is still in use in this Southern European kitchen (opposite).

A sturdy antique table takes pride of place in this working kitchen, where the original inglenook has been used to house the stove (above).

KITCHEN LAYOUT

KITCHEN PLANNING

Storage and display shelves, eating areas and space for food preparation are all vital elements in a successful country kitchen.

- *The kitchen, as the busiest room in the cottage, needs as much space as you can afford to give it. The conventional necessities – somewhere to store, prepare and cook food – should be arranged so that no part of the operation becomes a chore.*
- *An old-fashioned ceramic sink is not difficult to install, supported by stout brick piers which create useful storage space below. Position the sink beneath a window with a view and arrange generous and open worksurfaces, unshadowed by overhanging wall units, at either side.*
- *Old cupboards can be refaced with recycled boards to give a lived-in look to a kitchen. They provide different heights for work-surfaces made from tiles, marble, slate or wood.*
- *The country cooker which heats the house as well as the food is a welcome feature in any kitchen. Where the cooker has given way to an electric or gas replacement, a small wood-burning stove, used for warming winter soups and stews, can be a useful addition.*

KITCHEN STORAGE

Before the Industrial Revolution, the country cottage was a miniature factory where anything from clock parts to crab pots, and beer barrels to chair legs, was made.

The peasant family might work the landlord's land, but in between times there was cloth and wicker to weave, leather to be stitched, wax to be turned into candles. People's instinctive desire to create and construct from the natural materials around them had the added impetus of a wage, however small. A mixed economy was the life blood of a rural existence and the small country house was home and workshop rolled into one.

Many made space for their trade in the kitchen and slept contentedly with their stores of hemp or wool in the room next door. In the kitchen beside the spinning wheel, small tools, the musket and brass mortar, there would be the usual kitchen table and benches, cushioned stools and dripping pans, broiling irons and candle sticks. And set into the ceiling beams would be a collection of poles, pegs, nails, hooked chains, small shelves and racks where food, clothes and utensils hung in their allotted place above the cottagers' heads: a sharp knife for severing the kissing crusts between loaves welded together in the oven; a tin ladle for fishing the muslin herb bag out of the soup; a rack of spits set over the fireplace; a batch of buckets and pails hooked up beside a flitch of home cured bacon. In a modern country kitchen, the airing racks and beam hooks are still suspended from the ceiling and come in useful for hanging dried flower heads and a *batterie de cuisine*, bunches of lavender and strings of garlic. Storage and display are vital elements in creating a country atmosphere, while offering practical solutions for keeping utensils and china to hand. Dressers and shelves, freestanding and wall-mounted cupboards with solid or glass fronted doors, butchers' hooks and baskets, all provide ways in which to make the most of everyday china, kitchen utensils and precious ceramics.

Many an old kitchen contained no more furniture than would fit in a wheelbarrow, but the successful craftspeople put their money into improving their homes and furnishing their kitchens. An early investment was a locally built dresser, subsequently handed down from generation to generation.

Handed down from occupant to occupant were the built-in Cumbrian press cupboards which formed the wall between the kitchen and sleeping quarters downstairs. On the kitchen side there was storage for food like long-lasting rye loaves and oatcakes; on the bedchamber side there were linen shelves and clothes' hanging space. Other built-in cupboards were the salt box and the spice and herb cupboards set into the dry wall of the hearth, while freestanding or wall cupboards for food were placed away from the fire and ventilated with wickerwork sides or fronts.

American settlers took such designs with them or had local copies made in imitation of the originals. Others, like the Shakers, developed their own. The orderly kitchens of the Shakers included collections of cherrywood oval boxes to store everything from herbs and spices to buttons and nails. They refined this traditional design with its delicate tapering swallowtailed sides, and fitted lids which lifted off with a sigh, in pursuance of their creed 'Provide places for all your things, so that you know where to find them at any time, day or night'.

Today simple storage items like these displayed beside your favourite recipe books, well-worn chopping board, old kitchen clock, spice rack and pottery pieces contribute towards creative country kitchens.

STORAGE SOLUTIONS

The natural colours of this spartan stone kitchen in France (opposite above) are perfectly complemented by the simple cooking facilities offered by a two-ringed gas burner. Open shelves hewn from a former fireplace house china and pottery plates.

In the absence of an old-fashioned dresser, these modern wall cupboards with glass doors make effective display cabinets (opposite below left).

Copper griddles hang like decorative medals from these storecupboard doors (opposite below centre), while other polished copper jelly moulds and pans line the shelves.

Where space is at a premium, as in this Devon cottage (opposite below right), the kitchen table is sensibly set against a wall beneath a curtained storage cupboard.

KITCHEN DISPLAY

PLATES ON PARADE

Household objects on display in the country kitchen are often in regular use. Here, clay-coloured earthenware plate and dishes (left), both decorative and functional, are successfully complemented by a basic dresser which has been customized by the addition of crenellated edges on its shelves, while wooden slats are used as a backing.

Rather than exhibit a matching set of china, these open wooden shelves (opposite above), provide a platform for an assortment of glazed and painted plates, cups and dishes, together with a treasure trove of wooden and ceramic animals..

Simple collections, like these twelve spoons slotted into a painted wall rack (opposite below centre) can be used to break up a bare wall, while displays of treasured objects representing years of acquisition, can supply decoration for a whole wall.

Box shelving can be used to highlight compositions of collectables, each compartment highlighted by its own, individual stencil surround (opposite below left), while the bare stones of an old cottage wall provide an effective backdrop to a simple wooden stand weighed down with south European folk ceramics (opposite below right).

EATING AREAS

- *The art of creating agreeable eating areas is adaptability. A sound surface, a serviceable chair and congenial surroundings are all that are needed.*

- *The fashion for allocating a room solely for formal dining has diminished, but the need to create a relaxed eating area remains. The cottage convention was to enjoy fresh food as close as possible to the cooking activities.*

- *A broad and spacious kitchen can be created by removing partition walls between adjoining rooms, remembering to support load-bearing walls with a beam capable of bearing the weight.*

- *In such surroundings table and chairs form a natural division, especially when they can be placed under a sunlit window or in a well-lit corner, surrounded by a shelf display of decorative items.*

- *In smaller kitchens, a drop leaf table set against a wall will suffice for everyday use. It can be pulled out into the room to seat more when the occasion demands.*

- *There is no necessity to slavishly collect chairs which match the table – if three ladderbacks and two Windsors feel comfortable, they will persuade diners to linger just as long as would a matching set of antique chairs.*

TABLE MANNERS

The removal of a dividing wall, now supported by an elegant pale brick arch, has made a cool and calm dining area in this Umbrian farmhouse near Todi. A pink and white colour scheme diffuses the strong Italian light (above).

A collection of solid Scandinavian wooden table and chairs forms the main focal point in this simple interior (right).

Egen härd · Guld värd

AT THE TABLE

Social convention has turned full circle since the days when people shared their meal in the same room as it was cooked. After the post-war period, when kitchens seemed to be designed with the size of a telephone booth in mind and dining rooms were *de rigeur*, the kitchen has once again become the central room of the house and something of a status symbol.

No traditional country kitchen was complete without its modest collection of handmade furniture. A sound and solid table was often the most important piece, and the earliest examples were simple trestle tables or boards, made of rough-cut oak or elm; they were brought out at meal times and covered with a linen cloth which reached to the floor. Times changed and by the eighteenth century the trestle table had given way to gatelegged and folding tables or, in generous-sized kitchens, to broad oak tables which could seat a dozen people with ease. These days a pine table boasting bare boards is a popular option. The boards of an old table which bear the grazes and scratches of a long, hard life can be turned and sanded down. A weekly bleach scrub will keep the wood clean. Alternatively, a patterned oilcloth or waterproofed table cloth can be draped over the top, although pine and oak, unlike mahogany, will not be marked by a spill.

Nowadays, as in the past, the country dresser, lined with best plate and collections of country curios such as honey-pots or animal egg cups takes pride of place in the heart of the home. In the smaller kitchen, where work surfaces and storage space is limited, a work-surface island, made from a well-worn butcher's cutting block, or a small but sturdy old-wood table, can be used.

ROOM TO EAT

A wall of French windows opening directly onto the garden floods light into what would otherwise have been a sombre dining area. Dual-purpose rooms like these, furnished with favourite antiques and floored with hard-wearing tiles can be used for a range of purposes, from a children's playroom to a quiet study area.

WINING AND DINING

- *The greatest benefit of living in rural surroundings is the regular opportunity to exchange indoors for outdoors. An outdoor sun trap can be made by building a south-facing stone or block and whitewash wall, and flooring the area with paving slabs or old tiles. Break up the brightness with greenery, growing an espalier fruit tree or a vine against the wall.*

- *From the Cumbrian spinning galleries to the Italian* loggia*, many cottages incorporated a roofed area or gallery, open to the elements, for drying produce and fleeces or storing fuel.*

- *By tiling the floors, fitting slatted roller blinds and furnishing the gallery with appropriate furniture, these areas can be transformed into outdoor rooms, ideal for entertaining.*

- *Seasoned wooden benches and chairs made from wooden slats which drain off rainwater make serviceable outdoor furniture. Given an annual coat of timber preservative, they will forgive being left out all year round. Alternatively buy a basic picnic bench with fold-down bench seats.*

SIMPLE STYLE

Tempered by modern comforts, the austerity of the Shaker tradition holds this dining room in a balance between old and new (left). Simple whitewashed stone walls and the barrel ceiling provide a tranquil backdrop to the graceful candelabra and quilted wall hanging.

LOGGIA LIFE

Laid for the midday meal, a round table hides beneath a checkered table cloth (opposite above). Plain wooden chairs meet the needs of the diners who can enjoy their food beside a pretty paved area of the garden.

COOL TILES

A combination of timber, tiles and wrought iron furnish a relaxed dining area. Muslin drapes can be dropped across the windows to shield the diners from fierce sunlight, while the old cast-iron oven can still be lit with logs on a winter's night (opposite below).

KITCHEN FURNITURE

Early kitchen seating was confined to the stool or the settle. The three- or four-legged stool evolved into the backstool, where a solid or framed back support was added. This in turn developed into the enduring Windsor chair, with its sculpted seat and back rails often decorated with a wheel design.

In the mid-eighteenth century, when the sofa began to gain popularity among the well to do, the houseproud mistress would have been horrified to find such a luxurious item of furniture in the depths of the steamy kitchen. But the farmers' habit of keeping the old horsehair sofa close to the hearth has triumphed and under its new guise, the settle has returned to the country kitchen as an intrinsic part of informal family life.

GRACEFUL UTILITY

The use of natural materials is the hallmark of traditional country furniture. Wood, often worked while it was still green and pliable, would settle into shape as it seasoned and dried.

OUTHOUSES AND LAUNDRIES

From grand country houses to the pauper's cabin, it was a universal practice to pay more attention to the front of a house than to its rear. The finest ashlar stone and the best looking timbers were reserved for the public face of the house, while at the back, rough rubble or small wood was judged to be sufficient. And at the back of the cottage was the outhouse. Often a made-do-and-mend arrangement, the outhouse would be tucked under a cat slide roof of second-hand tiles or old shingles or, in Alpine regions, built as a timbered lean-to, nestling under the eaves of the chalet.

House sellers today call it the utility room. A couple of centuries ago they had as many names as uses for it. For some it was the brewhouse, cheese room and dairy, for others it was a buttery for wet stores such as ale and beer.

As a cold store the outhouse needed to be chilly. The back of the building was customarily the coldest side of the house and a stone flag or slate floor, a peephole sized window and a draughty stable door which lit the room and kept the dogs at bay, maintained a cool temperature on the sunniest of days.

The outhouse was equipped with storage containers according to need. One might hold a couple of barrels of cider, the smell of fermenting apples escaping with a hiss through a plug of straw. In some were stored the milk bowls, vats and presses for cheese making.

The outhouse was often the site of the salting bench on which the householder would lay sides of home-killed pig and laboriously rub in salt to make the meat keep. This particular process caused problems later in the life of the cottage as the salt penetrated the surrounding walls and caused damp.

In a few rare cases, and much to the envy of neighbours, the outhouse occasionally contained a water supply, either piped in from a nearby spring or delivered direct from a cast-iron hand pump set over a deep brick-lined well.

An indoor water supply meant that washing could be done in the outhouse and all the paraphernalia of the Monday wash – the dolly stool and mangle, the heating copper and the washboard – would share space with dried herbs such as lavender, *eau de cologne* mint and costmary, used to scent and moth-ball clean linen.

CULINARY COLLECTABLES

Utility rooms, traditional laundries and outhouses, while being a good location for functional items such as boilers, power meters and household appliances, often have space nowadays for collectable objects such as earthenware jars, cooking irons and china.

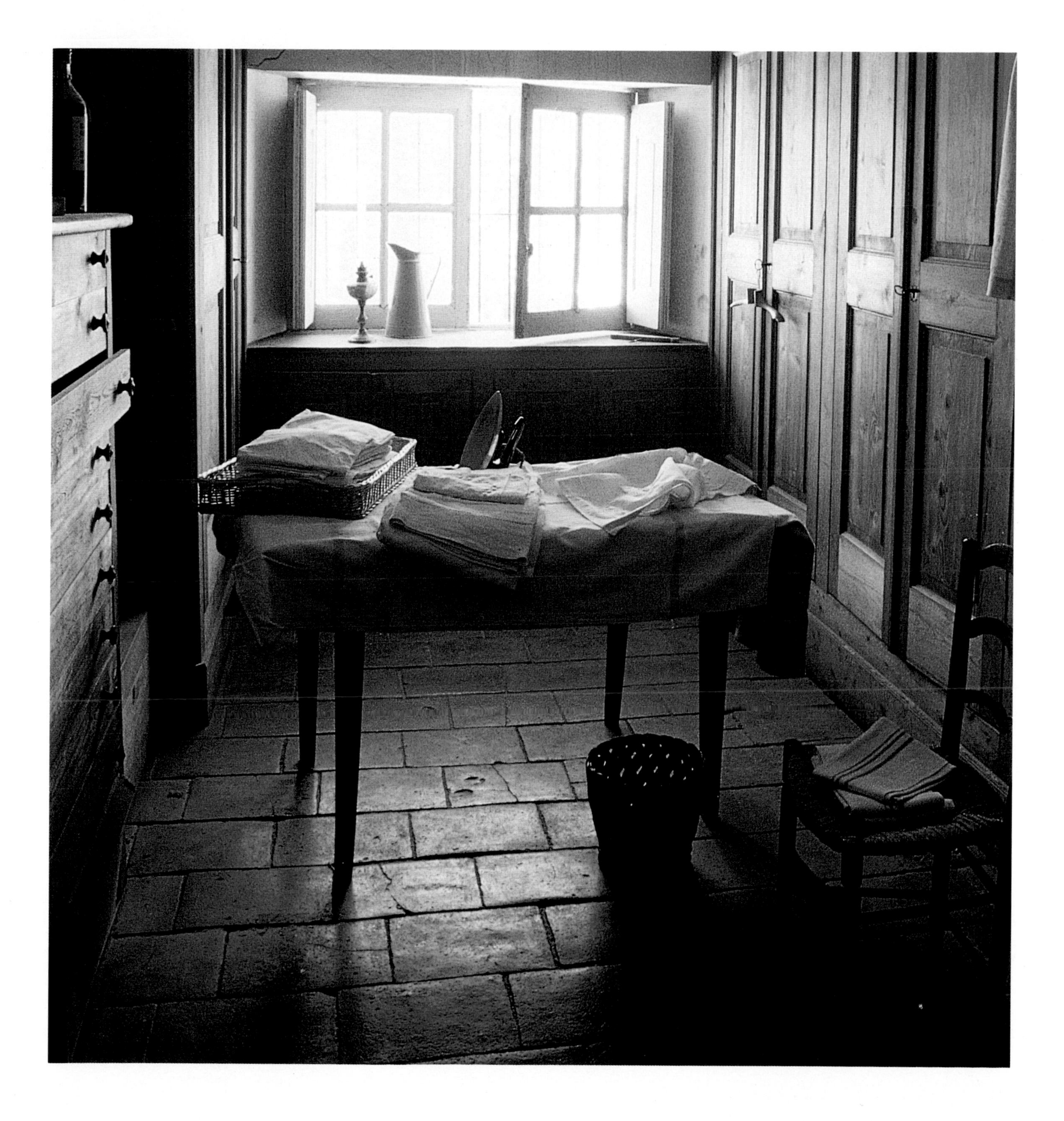

Chapter Three

ROOMS FOR LIVING

The perfect country living room should be a casual mix of natural materials and textiles, providing an immediate sense of comfort and a warm welcome. In the North, a blazing log fire, deep cushioned seats and the bold pattern of a kelim carpet are typical ingredients, while in the South, cool tiled floors, light, white walls and a summer breeze billowing against muslin curtains across an open door to the garden make a perfect Mediterranean living area.

The charm of the living room lies in its relaxed attitude to detail rather than to stylish contrivance. A place for eclectic collections of china, country textiles or antique kitchen implements, wall shelves, corner cupboards or over-sized log baskets, the living area should reflect personal taste but maintain tradition with vernacular furniture and an eye for simple, unfussy decoration.

LANGUID ELEGANCE

A conglomeration of natural materials in the living room makes for an unfussy, restful feeling. Here, luxuriously thick throws across the sofa, a collection of oriental cushion covers and a generous wickerwork log basket create an intimate atmosphere.

LIVING ROOMS

The living room does not have a long history since most cottages possessed no other living room than the kitchen. And yet most small country houses have one these days, so where did it come from?

If, during an informal cottage dinner party, some obtuse time machine were to reverse the clock by a century or so, guest and host would probably find themselves face to face with a benign cow chewing the cud and a roost of hens clucking in annoyance. The pretty hand-blocked wallpaper would be replaced by several coats of flaking whitewash, the deep, scroll-armed sofa by a single three-legged stool and the rich, walnut corner cupboard by a hay-filled stall. While kitchens have tended to stay in the same place, living rooms have been converted from what once would have housed the cottager's animals.

Most families were content with a large kitchen and an attic bedroom, provided the precious house cow and hens were under cover and close to hand. Until the nineteenth century, and in some parts of Europe until well into the twentieth century, the cottagers either stalled their livestock on the ground floor and lived above them, benefitting from the heat of the animals below, or else placed them at one end of the longhouse.

In Britain, the animals were being evicted to outside quarters from the nineteenth century on, as the commemorative datestones over many a stable and cowshed show. Faced with a new room to fit and furnish, the cottager had no option other than to follow the fashion for creating a drawing room or parlour.

Following the fashion of their better-off neighbours, as keenly as those neighbours would eventually copy their own cottage interiors, the parlour became the best room, furnished like a Victorian melodrama with dark drapes, an upright piano and a dark-stained dado below a cheap printed wallpaper. It was a place where children might play if they did so quietly and where the dead might lie before burial.

Such sombre surroundings did not last long in the cottage. The householder needed space for the burgeoning number of redundant articles from other parts of the house, and eclectic collections of old heating irons, butter pats, wooden decoys, china honey pots and tin animals nestled against those two items new to most cottages, wireless sets and book shelves.

Ironically, this was taking place as the style setters were hastily adopting the ideas of the Arts and Crafts movement, looking to juxtapose natural materials and textures with simple country furniture and solid-looking fireplaces.

Nowadays, cottage living rooms are often more spacious as a result of knocking down interior walls and combining two or three original rooms. In addition to storing and displaying collections, the atmosphere in a living room can be completely transformed by its furniture and soft furnishings. Floral fabrics create a traditional room, while upholstered chairs and sofas in plain fabrics make for a more formal drawing room. For simple sophistication, try combining checks and stripes in colours such as cool blue, yellow and terracotta.

Let the building itself guide you in your choice of decoration. While the clean lines of a Corbusier chair or an Art Deco table may look at home in the city, a cottage living room will be more comfortable if furnished with a traditional wooden rocking chair or a voluminous loose-covered armchair. Modern elements can be successful in an old building however, if used sparingly among older pieces.

BARED BEAMS

Usually concealed beneath plasterboard ceilings, the crafted complexity of this roof construction has been left exposed. Broad windows and wide doors prevent a top-heavy feel to the room.

RESTORING FEATURES

- *The older the cottage, the more difficult it becomes to identify original features. Rather than stripping the sound slate roof from your Breton croft and replacing it with an original reed thatch, concentrate on reinstating and exposing small vernacular details.*

- *Old fireplaces often lie hidden behind a wall of blockwork. Restore the open fireplace, substituting a cast-iron grate and firedog or an efficient wood-burning stove. Look out for (and lovingly restore) increasingly rare features like a lath and plaster firehood or indoor bread oven.*

- *Plasterboarding half-timbered ceilings prevented dust and dirt filtering through from the upper floor. Clear away the old plaster or plasterboard and seal the gaps between the beams with strips of new plasterboard.*

- *Wire-brush the beams and treat them with linseed oil to bring out their true, seasoned colour. Give the same treatment to timbered doorways, windowsills and wainscots.*

- *Internal walls of stone or wattle and daub survive beneath layers of ancient wallpaper. Expose a panel of walling, treating it with several coats of matt varnish to seal in the dust.*

PERSONAL REFLECTIONS

The character of any room will echo the personality of the current owner. Here (left), a strong sense of design as reflected in an eclectic collection of upholstered furniture, blends easily with the vernacular framework.

SUITABLY FITTING

Floral patterns and fine paintings complement the bare woodwork and stripped beams of a country living room (right). By integrating rather than superimposing their sense of design, the owners allow the room to retain its integrity.

COLOUR TREATMENTS

- *Light plays tricks with colour. Before committing a strong colour to an expanse of wall or ceiling, try a sample first on an area which will receive both artificial interior light and natural daylight.*

- *Old cottage wall surfaces (above), can vary from fresh plaster and brick to timber lintels and beams. Prepare surfaces like these by sanding down and priming fresh wood, repairing broken or crumbling plaster with cellulose filler, sanded smooth when dry, and by priming fresh plaster with a neutral emulsion paint, well watered down.*

- *Fashion is fickle with paint finishes, insisting on a particular finish one season and advocating the opposite view twelve months later. In reality, there is nothing new under the sun, only a kaleidoscope of colour schemes to be re-invented again and again.*

- *The addition of a* trompe-l'oeil *painting to raw or coloured plaster is an effective way of introducing colour, pattern and texture to a plain wall.*

- *This soft pink interior (right) has retained the traditional plaster finish on its gable wall, referring back to the days when, every spring, the cottage was given a fresh coat of whitewash inside and out in order to bear the next year's worth of stormy weather and sunshine.*

DECORATIVE DETAILS

- *Areas of contrasting or toning colour help to hold together a room's decorative scheme. Coordinated schemes do not need to be pedantic; the only thing which would jar in rooms such as these would be a badly crafted piece of furniture or an uncomfortable chair.*

- *Here a traditional soft yellow wash (left) provides a neutral background against which furniture and other objects are individually emphasized. A single paint colour carried across the narrow ceiling boards helps to pull the room together, while the use of different shades and complementary colours on features such as the high door arch, provides a colour counterpoint.*

- *Interiors like these, relying as they do on subtle colours and handmade furniture rather than an emphasis on a particular period of architecture, can be translated into a room of any age or any size. These fresh and simple Scandinavian bleached boards and ice-blue wall and ceiling colours in a living room (above right), are relieved by the polished warmth of a walnut writing desk and the darker tones of a dado rail, window frame and fire surround.*

- *The warm pastel pink shades applied between the dark fireplace and floor and the bright, white ceiling add warmth to this vernacular interior (below left). Water-based emulsions which are quick-drying and require no undercoat are ideal for wall coverings like these. Over-order your paint by half a litre (one pint) when using non-standard colours, so as to have a ready supply of the same colour for repainting later. Traditional oil-based paints in gloss, eggshell or satin finishes still give the best results on woodwork.*

- *Paint can also be used to highlight surface texture. In this room (below right), an old rubble wall has been deliberately rough-rendered and a gloss finish applied, to accentuate the patina.*

FINISHING TOUCHES

These colourful interiors display a close attention to detail, whether it be colour, texture or a careful selection of furniture.

FIREPLACES AND STOVES

The living room fireplace has been the central focus of the room from the time when a fire was no more than a pile of smouldering twigs and dried cow dung, to the smart modern substitute of a look-a-like, gas-powered log fire.

The original cottage fireplace, set centre stage in the middle of the room, was surrounded by low stools and benches, the ground-level seating arrangements made necessary by the smoke-filled rooms.

During the affluent English Elizabethan period, the start of what became known as the Great Rebuilding in Britain, fireplaces and hearths were built into walls. Positioning a fireplace in the centre of the old cottage, the chimney rearing up through the roof, divided the house into two distinct parts for the first time.

Although the rest of the house might be made of stone or timber, the chimney and fireplace was usually formed from brick. Used for cooking purposes, the fireplace was a cavernous affair with room for pots and pans hung from chains over the glowing embers. Some put a pine fire surround with a high mantelpiece above and set an earthenware bread oven or a chamber for smoking fish or meat into the side of the fireplace. Others favoured a broad lintel or bressumer, often of fire-resistant elm, to hold the chimney in place. A short skirt or curtain hung from the lintel to keep back the fire smoke. Beneath it an iron firedog or a log basket kept the blazing wood at bay while an iron fireback protected the back wall and radiated heat into the room. Firebacks were often heavily decorated – a favourite design was made by pressing pieces of rope and simple wood-carved designs into a sand mould before pouring the molten metal over the top.

In summer, the fireplace was filled with a decoration of dried flowers or pine cones or, especially in North America, covered with hand-painted fire boards which plugged the draught from the chimney.

In winter, the fire was lit again and kept alight until spring, although many a northern farmer claimed to have kept the house fire alight for a century or so.

The use of fossil fuels led to a new technology of fireboxes, raised hearths, grates and stoves, many of which were installed more for their good looks than for their efficiency. But in the cold north, the wood burning cast-iron or earthenware stove reigned supreme. The tall Scandinavian ceramic stoves, which heated stones stored in a tiled chamber over the fire, radiated warmth like night storage heaters, while the 'American' stove, which appeared in Pennsylvania in the early 1700s, drew in cold air from outside and breathed it into the living room.

Although central heating systems finally swept away the need for a central hearth, the open log fire and the wood stove have survived, providing the main focus for many a cottage living room. There are now myriad variations in the form of wood-burning stoves, simple wood surrounds, floral tiles or dramatic stone mantels.

COTTAGE INGLENOOK

When fireplaces like these (opposite above) were first built into the English country cottage, firewood was cheap and plentiful. Now, diminishing supplies emphasize the practicality of a more modest multi-fuel stove which, as the centrepiece of a cavernous stone inglenook, can become a feature in its own right.

UNREPENTANT LUXURY

The cushioned comfort of a chintz-covered sofa and chairs is enhanced by a blazing log fire (opposite below left). The log basket, fire bellows and dramatic candlestand hark back to the past and add a cosy ambience to enhance this meditative and comfortable living room.

FIRES WITHOUT FIREPLACES

Although it needs a chimney, the firebox and flue of a wood stove requires no fireplace (opposite below right). Such fires, set on a fireproof plinth of old bricks or tiles, create a heart-warming feature in any traditional cottage living room.

COUNTRY FURNITURE

The age of plastic, not to mention steel and nylon, has equipped us with the basic necessities of life, but the appeal of natural materials runs deep. Outside a museum of old buildings it would be difficult to find a dwelling furnished with nothing more than items made from wood, rush, reed and clay. And yet a century ago, the average cottager had no other alternative. It was a dependency that made him or her extraordinarily inventive.

The sparse furniture in a Hebridean cottage at the turn of this century might have run to a chest, some stools or logs for seats and, hung upon the wall, two or three wooden boards used as individual lap tables at meal times. The original family chests, sometimes carved out of a solid tree trunk, had one inherent disadvantage; the flat surface of the lid could not be used if the owner needed to be constantly rummaging around inside the chest. The court cupboard with open shelves over the closed storage space below overcame the problem. Tall enough to act as a room partition and frequently too large to be removed from the house without being dismantled, the seventeenth-century householder began to enclose the upper shelves to create the press-cupboard. Three hundred years later, country people in parts of Ireland still refer to their cupboards as presses.

Traditional furniture was made according to the customs of each region, but the ubiquitous dresser conquered all conservatism and was adopted right across the Northern world. Made of whatever materials were locally available, from Scandinavian pine to English oak, the dressers displayed bowls and cups, just as they do today.

The settle, the forerunner of the modern sofa, was similarly constructed of local wood, from ash, elm and birch to fruitwood, pine and deal. Here vernacular design resulted in a wide variety of styles including the 'seize' which looked more like an open-backed park bench, and the settle-bed.

MADE TO MEASURE

Most country cottages were once sparsely furnished and pride of place was given to a single fine piece of furniture.

DECORATED FURNITURE

The provincial fondness for colour, stronger in southern Europe than Britain, lead to a rich variety of painted furniture. In France, where graffitti artists still use stencils to make their mark, the *dominotiers* produced small painted papers or 'dominoes' bought by the boxful at the market and used as friezes on furniture. In America, journeymen artists roved amongst the East Coast settlers, overlaying bright pictures of birds and beehives, fruits and flowers on any and every surface, from the backs of rocking chairs and wooden cupboards to the living-room floorboards.

Vernacular styles, although unique to their own region, rarely developed in isolation. In the same way that the Iberian peninsular enjoys a Moorish influence, the Rococo and neo-Classical styles of France played a part in shaping the interiors of Scandinavian houses. Retained in rural homes long after the aristocracy had adopted new fashions, the spirited style of the traditional Scandinavian interior was imported to New England by the American settlers.

The abundant supplies of softwoods in both these countries were used to build the cottage and make its furniture. Paint, its pigments drawn from natural materials, provided protection and decoration.

Since the family bible was the only book liable to be found in most peasant homes, visual references for the furniture painter were limited to the natural surroundings. Itinerant painters were inclined to introduce fresh ideas into the remote settlements they visited, but the decorative tradition remained firmly rooted in folk art.

The art of stencilling which reached Europe from the Far East and Asia was also adopted by folk artists and both stencilling and painting furniture have enjoyed a revival.

Simple stencils, cut from acetate sheeting or oiled stencil boards, can be used to add colour to an otherwise featureless wall. On emulsioned wall surfaces, acrylics, poster paints or emulsion paints themselves work well.

Experiment with different paints on furniture; emulsions and diluted acrylics can be used with a protective top coat of tinted varnish. Prepare surfaces with as much diligence as you can muster and use a solid primer to seal the surface and key the decorative coats.

PAINTED DISPLAY

The habit of stripping pine furniture has made painted wall cupboards like these (left) comparatively rare until recently. This simply painted cupboard is enhanced by a display of bright glazed jugs.

SCANDINAVIAN BLUES

A blue-tiled corner stove (right) warms a room furnished with painted pieces. The manufacture of a longcase or a grandfather clock like this one standing on a decorated chest, was a traditional cottage industry.

COUNTRY SOFT FURNISHINGS

Traditional cottagers were no less fond of their creature comforts than we are today; they simply worked harder and longer to acquire them. The Shaker societies, for example, who pioneered the silk industry in Kentucky, raised their own silk worms, picked the cocoons, which yielded a mere pound of silk to a whole bushel of cocoons, and reeled, dyed and then wove the cloth themselves.

While most of the cottagers' soft furnishings were made for sale and a small profit, some at least remained in the home. Upholstered furniture might have been beyond the purse of the average cottager, but the product of the 'quishion loome' was not. These hay-filled cushions softened the impact of hard wooden country seats in the same way as foam box cushions and bolsters adorn window seats today, while linen drapes, embroidered wall hangings and lace curtains, each according to the local style, were also found in country homes.

Before the Industrial Revolution, the very materials for soft furnishings came from the garden and beyond. Irish linen rose from fields of white flax and Welsh wool from the sheep grazing beside the blackberries, elderberries and cow parsley that were used to dye their fleeces.

Thankfully, contemporary soft furnishings involve nothing more labour-intensive than choosing a fabric, although the plethora of fabrics and designs on the market now make choosing colours and themes a daunting task if you are starting from scratch.

Furniture and architectural features are not the only medium for soft furnishings in the living room. Large baskets, traditionally used for storing logs, may be embellished with simple gingham fabric, loosely sewn around their top edge and tied in an informal knot – a perfect home for children's toys or untidy newspapers and magazines.

DEEP-SEATED COMFORT

The formal panelling of this small living room is softened by a deep and comfortable sofa filled with delicately decorated cushions.

WINDOW TREATMENTS

- *Find out what kind of window treatments would be historically accurate for your cottage and then decide whether to copy them exactly or whether to experiment a little.*
- *A decision which will affect the overall feel of a living room is whether to opt for traditional curtains – with pelmets, frills and tie-backs in chintzy fabric – or to choose simple gingham checks or muslin drapes.*
- *If you choose bold, colourful fabric for your curtains, use calico to upholster chairs and sofas, and treat it as a blank canvas on which to decorate, adding bold cushions and throws to echo the colour, pattern and texture of your curtains.*
- *On small windows, think about using simple lace drapes or classic Roman blinds as an alternative to curtains.*

CAUGHT IN THE WIND

A tasselled gingham curtain catches the breeze in a diminutive cottage window (right).

CAFE CURTAINS

Hung halfway up a cabin window, these plain yellow café curtains reduce the window height but allow natural light to flow freely (left).

COUNTRY CRAFTS AND TEXTILES

Following on from the nineteenth-century factory boom which not only swept away cottage crafts, but removed the craftspeople themselves from the country to the towns, there has been a steady revival in recent years of rural, handmade articles as carpet makers, iron masters, glass blowers, clock makers, potters, weavers and clog makers move out of town once more to set up country businesses.

Whether the view from the cottage window was a Mediterranean olive grove or the heathered hillsides of a Yorkshire moor, the old country house invariably contained some example of the cottage crafts. There were precious few ornaments to be had apart from what the cottagers made themselves. Many items were utilitarian – painted tin coffee pots, copper warming pans, cane carpet beaters and decorated herb choppers. Other items were kept for their spiritual insurance value. Horse brasses were hung from the mare's harness to ward off the evil eye, while corn dollies, plaited from the last sheaf of the harvest and felled by the reapers' thrown sickles, were displayed to ensure a good harvest in the year ahead.

In the Finnish province of Karelia where the landworkers lived together in their timbered farmhouses, anyone entering the living room bowed first to the religous icon set in the corner and then to the pagan horse's head set by the hearth. They also used the horse's head as a device for sorting yarn.

Carpets and rugs were traditionally made, if not by the householder themselves, then by some local craftsperson whose fees were judged to be lower than their talents. Not that carpets appeared in many cottages before the late nineteenth century. The present abundance of both carpets and rugs on the floors of the contemporary cottage is a new phenomenon. Two centuries ago, carpets covered tables, rugs covered beds and floor cloths covered floors.

The floor cloth was a piece of canvas or oil cloth often painted to mimic the knots of floor boards or the pattern of floor tiles, like the linoleum floor coverings which replaced them in the mid nineteenth century. In the Americas too, carpets were a rarity and bare, varnished or simply painted floorboards the rule. When, in the late nineteenth century, the Shakers started to relax their attitude towards ornamentation, they began to manufacture rugs and knitted carpets.

Straw, cane and rush mats were more common in the south, while rugs were prevalent in the north. One thickly textured version involved weaving strips of coloured rag tied together through a strong warp of woollen yarn. The hooked rug which probably originated in Scandinavia (rug comes from the Swedish *rugg* or rough hair) was variously known as a clootie or stobbie in northern Britain. The clootie was made by looping strips of rag through a coarse canvas backing or a redundant potato sack.

WARM CURTAINS

Handmade textiles created from locally available materials would once have been the only form of soft furnishings in a country cottage. Ornamentation did not become an integral part of the cottage interior until the late nineteenth century.

DISPLAYS

The contemporary cottage living room would not be complete without its fair share of collected treasures, whether they be painted ceramics displayed neatly on a set of wooden shelves, copper pans suspended from oak beams or watercolour paintings hung on walls.

Colour plays an important role in any display, so think about the backdrop before embarking on any painting or decorating. Vivid blue-painted shelves against a mint green wall for example, could make for a distracting mix of colours. Similarly, if you want to display a collection of pale yellow china, think carefully about which background colour would show it off to best effect.

Where possible, make full use of any existing nooks and crannies in the room for display. Redundant serving hatches, stone window recesses and generous sills all have potential as display areas for prized possessions.

Other means of displaying objects include traditional dressers, which can be used for storage too, built-in alcove shelves and cupboards and, of course, mantelpieces and inglenook fireplaces.

Built-in cupboards and shelves were regularly incorporated into country homes to serve as herb shelves, salt boxes and food stores (right). The alcove on this English cottage wall has been turned into a trompe-l'oeil *with an arched hood and a pair of painted shutters (above).*

Chapter Four

SLEEPING QUARTERS

Sloping rafters, low ceilings and an economical use of limited roof space create country cottage bedrooms which are warm, snug and simple. Cottage bedrooms often occupy the loft area, where the morning light once lit upon stores of fruit and grain spread across the attic floorboards. When, in the nineteenth century, the cottager began to copy the example of his more affluent farmer neighbours and converted this storage space into bedrooms, boxbeds and settles gave way to cast iron and brass beds, which called for an increased sense of comfort, while cotton counterpanes and colourful quilts replaced sheepskins and furs. Popular taste led to the introduction of wooden washstands and china water jugs, bedside rugs and floral curtains.

If the provision of separate bedrooms was late in coming to the old cottage, the arrival of the bathroom was even later, but these days the cottage mood has extended into both the bedroom and bathroom. Rarely grand and seldom lavish, country bedrooms and bathrooms should be, above all else, modest, cheerful and cosy.

SOUND SLEEPING

The muted pink plaster paint finish of this Scandinavian bedroom is enhanced by a delightful trompe-l'oeil *of garden flowers and a painted swag at picture rail height. Bleached floorboards blend effortlessly with the rough-painted chair and side table.*

BEDROOMS

The medieval habit of sleeping by the fireside was still widespread in Europe a hundred years ago. Bedcupboards, settle beds and even a plain slab of stone set into the side wall of the kitchen served the sleepers, but once the cottager decided that sleeping in the kitchen would no longer do, different bedrooms were made to suit different cottages.

Those reluctant to leave the warmth of the main room built a bedroom annexe directly off the kitchen, scarcely bigger than the family bed itself. Common in North America and Northern Ireland, the annexe was often insulated with a ceiling of woven grass or rush matting and later with old newspapers pasted across the ceiling and concealed beneath a coat of whitewash.

Building bedrooms upstairs depended on the shape of the cottage roof. On bare, windswept heaths and open, coastal plains, the cottage kept its head down low and roof space was minimal. In the kinder lowlands, where there was a good living to be made from the land, the two-storey cottage was commonplace.

In highland areas where long winters and deep snowfalls were customary, roofs were sharp pitched and steep, allowing for a warren of upper-floor rooms to be slipped easily into the roof space.

In larger cottages, a stone staircase wound up around the back of the hearth to reach the loft above, or was inserted as a steep flight of wooden steps leading straight up from the kitchen into the loft space. Lit by a pair of tiny dormer windows at floor level, the loft could be divided into a balcony bedroom which led on to a second, enclosed room. Sharing space with the stores of apples, fleeces or grain, the best bed would be stood over the heated kitchen below. One typical version was to have a divan built above the warm charnel, a raised recess in the kitchen ceiling used to hang bacon and herbs.

Some cottages, like the Welsh *crogloft*, were too small even for a stairway. (Being a land of small houses, the Welsh language contains as many different words for a small house as the Eskimos have names for snow.) The *crogloft* possessed two ground-floor rooms, a kitchen open to the rafters and a parlour, with a bedroom squeezed in over the parlour. Again, a straw or rush woven ceiling insulated the little bedroom and a loft ladder, rather than a staircase, led up to the bed.

Cottage bedrooms today should encourage rest and relaxation, be neither too chintzy nor too strident in their decoration, and reflect the traditional country elements of decoration – soft colours combined with a variety of natural textures and materials.

Here, as elsewhere in the home, hand-crafted rugs, furniture and fabrics would once have been the only form of embellishment and storage, so think about traditional forms of decoration when planning your bedroom scheme. Individual chests of drawers and wardrobes are preferable to built-in units in the country bedroom, as are individual beds rather than mass-produced divans. Keep fabrics simply floral or subtly checked, and consider your requirements for privacy or light at the windows. Delicate lace or muslin drapes look entirely at home in the country bedroom, but remember to think about whether you need to keep out noise or bright sunlight before consigning your thicker curtains to the obscurity of the blanket box.

LYING IN LUXURY

The grandeur of this four-poster bed draped with white curtains is matched only by the direct view of the garden from the bedroom door. A generous lace-like curtain affords the room some privacy.

BEDROOM LAYOUT

Restrained simplicity and the use of traditional furniture and furnishings have turned this spare bedroom (left above) into a welcome retreat. From the local quilt and rag rug to the blanket chest, wooden bed and ledge-and-brace door, the basic elements combine to recreate a cosy and straightforward country style based on natural materials.

Use of light is important, especially in country surroundings where natural daylight is usually in abundance. On one side of a building, windows will open onto muted sunsets; on the other, to the clear light of dawn. By taking over a corner room with windows on two sides, this bedroom (left below) catches the late evening light and gives a bright start to the day, while the tiled stove set against one wall is guaranteed to take the chill off the morning air. Pleasantly spacious rooms like these can double as living or work rooms.

A glimpse into the sleeping quarters of the average country cottage a century ago would reveal a tiny room tucked in under the eaves of the house. Nowadays, bedrooms are often rooms that have been converted from former living areas.

Here two ground-floor bedrooms exhibit on the one hand a cool and elegant decorative scheme and, on the other, a congenially snug option: a pair of black iron bedsteads (above left) stand on terracotta tiles in a calm, cream room. On cold nights the fire in this former living room can be lit to add a touch of luxury.

Similarly (left below) the imposing fireplace in this former kitchen has been retained and now forms the central focus of the room. The stable door which opens directly onto the garden, the cottage washstand and the handy fireside cupboard express a delightfully traditional cottage feel.

BEDS

The current expectation that we spend a third of our life in our beds did not hold true in the past when the working day began at dawn or sooner. Nevertheless the cottager expected to sleep in some comfort.

Social division kept the impoverished in their place, but the demand for servants gave the less affluent an insight into the sleeping habits of the wealthy. Seeing that the rich slept on feather or combed wool mattresses, cocooned in their curtained four-poster beds, the poor were less inclined to hold fast to their traditional straw mattresses and old-fashioned bed cupboards.

An aspiring yeoman farmer might install a passable reproduction of an Elizabethan four-poster complete with drapes and curtains. The headboard sometimes contained a small cupboard and there would certainly be an additional ledge or shelf on which to stand the candle or rushlight, with its attendant fire risks.

But in the small country cottage space was at a premium. A truckle bed, like a low divan on wheels, could be stored during the day beneath the main bed. Then there was the press bedstead, which folded up to resemble a chest of drawers, and the more useful settle bed, popular in North America and Ireland which, like the sofa bed, folded into a seat or low sideboard. Another portable bed was the rope bunk, made by stringing cords between the headboard and footboard and tightening them against a bedboard at night.

The Breton and Scandinavian box- or cupboard-bed was economic with both heat and space. Often made with the children's bunk above the parental bed, the front and sides were decorated with painted wooden panels while woollen hangings on curtain rails could be closed during the night to keep in the warmth. Others, built into the cottage wall beside the hearth, were closed off in the day by a pair of panelled doors which formed the back of the fireside settle.

In warmer climates the cottagers slept on half-headed or stump beds, with a plain headboard at the top end. The mattress was laid across a web of rush or rope straps, with a rush or canvas mat between the webbing and the mattress. Gradually, the forged iron bedstead, already in use in Italy, and the brass bedstead, with springs replacing the old webbing, gravitated down through the social classes in the eighteenth and nineteenth centuries.

The most expensive traditional mattresses were filled with swan's down, while the cottager's economy version would be filled with heather, animal hair and even beech leaves. Additional mattresses were used for extra comfort – in the seventeeth century Cardinal Wolsey expected to find no less than eight beneath him. While textile crafts remained a cottage industry, good linen and blankets or fleeces covered the beds, together with the traditional bedcover and the handcrafted patchwork quilt, which added a bold dash of decorative colour and texture to the cottage bedroom.

BOX BEDS

This fine example of a box bed has a sleeping space behind the curtains as well as a bunk bed above. Once common throughout Scandinavia, northern France and Britain, the box bed can still provide serviceable sleeping arrangements for young children.

BEDS AND BEDDING

- *A good bed will not last forever, but given a good mattress and a sympathetic choice of bedlinen, the traditional beds shown here are as comfortable as they are good-looking. This American wooden bed (left), with its dramatically tall turned posts and deep mattress, is covered with a traditional quilt.*

- *Large family beds were seldom found in smaller country cottages, but settle beds such as this green painted example from Finland (below far left) provided the ideal solution. By day they were used as a bench seat and by night, with a straw, heather or combed wool mattress, they served the sleeper well enough.*

- *Metal bedsteads (below left) became a classic country cottage design, only to be abandoned in the early twentieth century. Many have been exhumed from the bottom of the garden to be fully restored with a gleaming new coat of paint.*

- *This iron bedstead (right above) has been finished off with an elevated lace-edged valance to complement the white bedcover. Light lace bedding (below right) provides an effective contrast to a carved bedhead in dark wood. Another traditional bed, the north European cot (below far right), is enhanced with fretwork carvings at the head and feet.*

QUILTS

Long before quilting reached a pinnacle of popularity among polite circles in the eighteenth-century reign of the English Queen Anne, cottage women were using their quilting skills to make essential household items such as bedspreads and clothing. In the subsequent three centuries the tradition was kept alive by American settlers and by other Europeans.

Dusting their work-grimed fingers with talcum powder, women sewed, stitched and embroidered their fabric oddments, turning them into sheets of colour. Such work was an important part of the cottage economy. In the, days before the American weaving industry had established itself and imported cloth was expensive, no scrap of fabric was left to waste.

Among the traditional soft covers made by cottagers were fine-stitched white quilts stored in the press cupboard until needed for the laying out of the dead; lightweight linen sheets decorated with embroidery or appliqué to serve as summer quilts and heavier serge cloth backed with brown paper and flannel to provide extra warmth in the winter; quilted woollen counterpanes covered with an extra quilt, buttoned on for appearance sake; petticoats, table cloths, settle covers, pillows, mats and cushions – the cottagers' ingenuity was limited only by supplies of thread, fabric and a workable amount of daylight.

Work often began after the traditional spring clean, and continued until the summer light began to wane. Quilt-making was a practical way to teach children to sew and patterns have been handed down from mother to daughter for generations. Organized working sessions, known as quilting bees, brought women together to work on a quilt that was to be presented to one of their sisters as a traditional wedding present.

But quilting was not confined to the womenfolk. There were professional quilters and markers – people who marked out quilt designs – who journeyed between communities, living off their skills. One of those was Joe the Quilter, murdered in his Northumberland cottage in 1862, a victim of the local gossip that quilting had made him a rich man. Like other country craftspeople, Joe was as poor as his neighbours, and the perpetrators, who were never found, went away empty handed.

Like the European emigrants who took the quilting skills to the New World, travelling quilters did much to export regional designs. While the craft flourished in North America, it was also celebrated in small parishes of the north of England, Wales and Ireland, especially those with a mining community such as Durham, Northumberland and the Welsh valleys.

Good design involves plans, working drawings and experimentation. The making of the family quilt did not. The utilitarian quilt evolved as work progressed, although the use of wooden or tin templates and repeated traditional motifs like tulips, feathers and hearts gave the quilt worker control over the finished product. But there were superstitious dangers to be considered: breaking the cable design bordering a wedding quilt was thought to be an ominous sign for the couple's future, so great care was taken over the finer details of these special quilts.

QUILT MAGIC

Embroidery and the making of patchwork quilts were major forms of domestic folk art on both sides of the Atlantic. Quilts not only warmed the sleeper but were worn as clothing throughout the eighteenth century. Later on, they became a symbol of marriage. An American girl would expect to have thirteen quilts in her hope chest, the thirteenth being her own bridal quilt.

Designs like these (opposite) were drawn from nature. Patterns in the shape of oak leaves, turkey tracks and the crown of thorns were especially popular.

Another favourite quilting design was the lily pattern (left), seen here on a traditional American colonial bed.

BEDROOM FABRICS

BEDROOM FABRICS

Soft furnishings in the country bedroom should be uncomplicated. Try using natural fabrics in a combination of simple colours and patterns such as cool lemon and blue checks and ginghams or gentle florals on a white ground.

Curtains look more homely if they are full length, adding a sense of luxury to simple surroundings.

Bedcovers and bedlinen should blend or contrast with your chosen decorative scheme, while cushions, bolsters and throws can lend extra colour interest to large beds.

On this lightweight version of the traditional tester, or four-poster bed (left), white sheer curtains enclose the bed at night. A deep valance and a fabric skirt over the bedside table complement the bed curtains.

A white bed drape edged with pink bobble trim (below left) defines the bed space against the pink wall of this rural bedroom. Similarly (below right) a bed is framed by deep white lace drapes hung from the ceiling above a narrow bed embellished with carved bedheads. These show off the fabric to good effect.

An American field bed (opposite) complete with a delicate arched tester draped with a netted coverlet takes pride of place in this simply defined bedroom.

BEDROOM STORAGE

In the typical high ceilinged homes of southern Europe free standing cupboards or wardrobes are ideal for storage. Make room for them by situating beds in the centre of the room or beneath draught-proofed windows.

While old beds were built for generations of people who were generally shorter than we are today, old wardrobes were constructed to take long, flowing dresses and suits. Increase their internal storage space by adding in an extra rail.

Curtain off alcoves with drapes which match the wall colours, suspended from a wooden curtain rod or bamboo rail. Open shelving and clothes-hanging space can be built in behind the curtains, while the gap between the curtain rail and ceiling can become a display shelf for a collection of wooden colonial suitcases or hatboxes.

For the sake of making the room rectangular, large areas of space are lost beneath the roof space. Open an alcove into the roof space, extending the bedroom floor to cover the new area and expose roof trusses, setting insulation and plasterboard strips between them. Line the opening with wardrobe rails and hooks or open shelves.

Grand four-poster beds used to have storage compartments set into the headboard of the bed. Embrace the old idea by framing the bed head with cupboards, running them over the top of the bed. Standard fitted cupboards may not suit the cottage look of a room; use old or recycled wood instead and give it a distressed paint finish with contrasting coats of matt emulsion, roughly rubbed down to reveal random patches of undercoat.

SCANDINAVIAN SPLENDOUR

Voluminous and intricately painted wardrobes frame the doorway of this simple but imposing wooden interior.

NATURAL MATERIALS

A floor-to-ceiling gentleman's dresser is perfectly complemented by huge baskets containing dried branches. The wooden floor tones well with the natural colours and textures of the furniture.

PAINT EFFECTS

Cottage history only began to be properly documented in the late nineteenth century. Although careful observations have been made of construction methods, of vernacular furniture and furnishings, the movement was too late to record more than a fragment of traditional painting practices. What little is left has been pieced together from faded remains.

The basic paint ingredients were the pigment and the medium, the former made from natural and artifical ingredients, the latter from vegetable or animal sources like linseed oil for oil paints or water for distemper.

Distemper was the most frequently used treatment for cottage walls and white the most common colour. Whitewash and limewash, made with slaked lime, were generously coated on walls, inside and out – and often on the thatched roof as well, since it was believed to act as a fire retardant.

Early painters ground their own pigments, mixed their own paints and jealously guarded their recipes. But popular pigments such as red and yellow ochres, pale blue verdigris and a lime blue made from sulphate of copper, were open secrets and used as local fashion dictated. Paint treatments

were as bold and imaginative as the available materials allowed and included waist-high bands of red ochre; lemon green and deep blue ceilings and walls; artificial graining and marbling of walls; and wainscots covered with oil paint or decorated with trailing vines, leaves and flowers.

The restoration of a country cottage will occasionally reveal old traces of paintwork – bright floral or zig-zag designs painted on beams or dainty frescos, where paint was applied to plaster while it was still wet – hidden beneath layers of wallpaper. Such discoveries will be rare and unique.

HOMESPUN HUES

A distemper colour wash was the traditional treatment for the rough plastered walls of most country cottages such as this one (opposite). Colouring agents included natural elements such as bullock's blood, soot, charcoal and plant extracts.

FLORAL EMBELLISHMENT

Cottage exteriors were simple and unadorned, but the cottager was no less fond of interior design than today (above). The discovery of an old fresco or wall painting is a cause for celebration and careful restoration.

COUNTRY BATHROOMS

The history of the cottage bathroom is brief. Modern baths, basins and showers were of little use in a home where the water supply relied on the contents of the rain-water barrel and the backyard well. Until the early twentieth century, the tin bath, the chamber pot and the garden privy, or the 'little house' at the end of the garden, serviced country families well enough. The tin bath or the hip bath, particularly recommended for the relief of saddle soreness, hung by a peg in the outhouse until needed. On bath nights, it was stood before the kitchen fire, filled up with cauldrons of hot water and used by each member of the family in turn before being emptied with a bucket at the end of the evening.

When bathrooms began to be installed towards the end of the nineteenth century, they were placed in the smallest room of the house, frequently on the ground floor and often at the back. Here, on the cold side of the building, many have remained, but, bearing in mind that bathrooms are subservient to their fixtures and must be plumbed into the drainage system, many new owners sensibly choose to move the bathroom to a more pleasant position. Country cottages generally enjoy a good view and certainly see more of the sun than their urban counterparts so provided the bathroom window affords some privacy, by means of a café curtain or a translucent Roman blind, one which looks out on the sunny side of the garden is a welcome improvement.

Like kitchens, bathrooms have to function well around a layout dictated by fixed fittings. But with no traditional model on which to base their designs, householders can let their creative imagination run wild in designing a room which is as comfortable as it is practical.

Cork floors, or a thick cork floorboard to cushion bare feet against a terracotta tiled floor; soft, indirect lighting; and sun-warm colours and waterproof wall finishes, in tiles or softwood boarding, all work well. Floor-to-ceiling boarding could give the bathroom a pine-heavy look, while tongue-and-groove boards, painted to match walls and ceiling, can be run up to windowsill height to box-in pipework to the bath, basin and cistern. The wall shelf created by the boarding provides a useful all-round surface to display curiosities such as a piece of twisted driftwood or a simple vase filled with dried grasses, together with the inevitable clutter of shampoo bottles and toothbrushes.

Building narrow shelves and discreet cupboard doors into the boardwork can also create useful storage spaces for bathroom paraphernalia and towels, as will a recycled wooden washstand or an old rushwork laundry basket.

COOL RETREATS

Cottage bathrooms are often planned from scratch, providing the houseowner with the opportunity to create a room which is refreshingly decorated in neutral tones.

The ideal bathroom as defined by one architect is a room where you can feel comfortable when naked; if the bathroom fails to conform to this description, remodel it or remove it to a warmer, lighter situation.

If you have inherited a miniature bathroom, look for space-saving ideas; could the bath be re-sited in a roomy bedroom and a shower set in its place? Would a mirrored wall impart a lighter, more airy feel to the room? Could a sunken bath and shower, set against the far wall, solve the problem?

Opt for warming effects in a chilly, oversized bathroom: a cushioned floor, an old-fashioned cast iron radiator painted red, luxurious velvet curtains and a sympathetic colour finish. Replace white tiles with hot Mediterranean glazes or paint over the old tiles with a coat of eggshell yacht paint, followed by a warm gloss.

Replace the old bath with a more modest-sized substitute, projecting it into the room rather than parking it conventionally along one wall. Use tongue-and-groove panelling up to waist height, painted to match the walls. Introduce a dressing table and a pair of coloured rattan chairs and bring back wooden venetian blinds, which let in light yet maintain a sense of privacy.

A spacious bathroom can take a large and luxurious bath, free-standing on its claw feet, but a smaller three-quarter length bath, which is more economical with water, can be just as effective boxed-in with recycled mahogany floorboards.

As with any other room, it is the fine details which give a sense of character. Cane baskets and candles, green plants and driftwood, seashells and sailing boats – let your imagination run riot.

TILE STYLE

A beautifully bizarre collection of tiles creates a spirited pattern on this bathroom wall. The painted bath, set out into the room, takes full advantage of available space, while the carpet adds a touch of luxury.

BATHROOM PLANNING

● *Condensation and steam are perennial problems in small, poorly ventilated bathrooms. Water corrodes old brickwork and plaster and leads to the kind of indoor vegetation which no one welcomes. Treat old walls with a waterproofing agent or line them with a damp-proof membrane and plasterboard and provide the room with a free flow of air by adding a window or door fanlight. Here the solution was to resurface the walls in seagreen wood panelling to incorporate a useful shelf along one wall.*

● *Beneath the plastered walls of many timber-framed homes lies the elegant skeleton of the house itself. By exposing the woodwork and plastering or plasterboarding the spaces between the timber panels you can restore the framing to its former glory.*

● *The nineteenth-century fashion for blacking old beams has persisted, but they can be wire brushed or sand blasted down to their original, natural colour. These dark beams framed against the white plaster go well with the dark red bath and furnishings, providing a weathered backdrop.*

● *Planning out a new bathroom needs careful consideration. Use scale plans for both the room and its fittings to ensure an economical use of space and a practical layout for laundry baskets and towel rails.*

● *Small rooms might need features such as sliding doors and built-in storage cupboards; larger rooms can accommodate extra individual items of furniture such as a freestanding wardrobe or a* chaise longue.

This handsome blackwood and marbled washstand fits well into this simply tiled bathroom in Southern France.

● *Bringing the bath out from the wall allows the bather to enjoy the full effect of a window with a view. Positioning shelves or cupboards close to the bath puts shampoos and lotions conveniently within arm's reach.*

● *In this pale yellow room with its tongue-and-groove boards, natural coir matting and distinctive blue bath, there was room to include the old cottage washstand, while wall-to-ceiling cupboards provide all the storage space that is needed. Washstands make practical and classic additions to bathrooms where there is space for them.*

Chapter Five

THE COTTAGE GARDEN

A good cottage garden should amount to more than the sum of its parts. It may include a shrub-fringed lawn, a path edged with flowers or a productive vegetable plot, but its totality goes beyond the purely horticultural. The asparagus bed will feed the body and the bougainvillea in flower will feed the eye, but the garden as a whole also has the power to feed the soul.

From its modest origins as a randomly planted plot of vegetables and its overabundance of easily cultivated, low-maintenance flowers such as roses, hollyhocks and honeysuckle, the contemporary cottage garden often boasts an amalgamation of traditional formality and freeform planting. By mixing a formal layout of herbs, for example, with areas of haphazard planting, such a garden can combine the restrained with the untrained to create separate 'rooms' of colour, texture and atmosphere that are both useful and decorative.

DISCREET ORDER

In the apparent chaos of the country garden, discreet order reigns. Amongst the profusion of foxgloves, sweet williams, poppies, mallow and cornflowers lining the gravel path, each plant has its allotted place. Many of these classic flowers were once grown specifically for culinary or medicinal uses.

LOCAL LANDSCAPES

Early cottage gardens were practical, productive units, their plants grown as much for medicinal and superstitious reasons as for culinary purposes – lavender repelled fleas and bistort kept away disease, while house leeks protected against lightning and a rowan tree was a defence against witchcraft.

The spirit of recycling thrived as plants were propagated and seeds were collected and saved. There was a healthy exchange of plants between gardeners who worked for the grand country houses and their more modest neighbours in the village. But, unlike the manor or château gardens with their contrived landscapes and formal designs, the cottage garden had no set planting pattern; plants grew in profusion but with a purpose. Herbs were especially popular country plants, being both useful and decorative: scented hyssop was strewn across the cottage floor; angelica and rosemary seed, after cooking over a slow heat, perfumed the house, and lemon balm was used to polish and scent oak furniture.

In the Mediterranean lowlands, many gardens remain as they were several centuries ago. Devoted to fruit and vegetable cultivation and the rearing of livestock, the Mediterranean cottager practised a sustaining rotation of grazing and fallow land which enriched the soil and established a healthy ecological balance. The fallow land, freckled with flowering meadow herbs served as a lawn; an intensively cultivated kitchen garden supplied the household with fresh vegetables; while sheep and hens kept down the grass in the orchard.

In Britain especially, the cottage gardener gradually began to grow plants for their good looks alone. By the early 1900s, the traditional cottage grounds, with their profusion of hollyhocks and roses and neat rows of onions and peas, became a recognizable pattern, repeated all over the country, providing inspiration for international garden designers.

In time, a two-way exchange of ideas resulted in the cottage garden being influenced by grander gardens. Features of formal gardens such as the hedged kitchen garden, the leisurely sward, the rose-bowered pergola and topiared trees have been scaled-down and incorporated into the cottage garden. No longer confined to densely packed, informal flower borders, the small garden can these days incorporate a range of landscapes in miniature – woodland and water gardens, rock and rose gardens, *parterre* and parkland – without losing its integrity.

The making of a good garden requires only time and hard work and the rewards are immeasurable. Even if householders hard-pressed for time do no more than keep the weeds at bay and import the occasional tray of geraniums from the village market each spring, they will still find themselves working with nature and enjoying it. The rural landscape is a patchwork quilt of fields, woods, heaths and hillsides stitched together by handmade boundaries of hedges, ditches and stonewalls. The last half century has transformed it almost beyond recognition. Altered to make the business of farming more efficient, small fields have been merged into prairie-sized units, moorlands have been ditched, drained and put to the plough, and woodlands felled and turned to grazing land. The changes, instituted to reduce the labour force and mechanize the farming process, have had a more radical effect on the look of the land than anything which has occurred in the past two hundred years.

For much the same reasons, cottage gardens mirrored the new age. In the early post-war years, garden design books advocated layouts which were easy to maintain, neat and dull. The labour-intensive vegetable plot was put down to grass, orchards were rationalized to make way for the riding mower, and flower beds were shrunk to manageable sizes.

But the charm of the countryside lies in its variety; secretive lanes threading their way past hedgerowed meadows, old tracks meandering through ancient but productive woods, a stone packhorse bridge crossing an unkempt stream. Saddened by this loss of local diversity and spurred on by the spirit of conservation, many cottage gardeners have begun to recreate the variety of the countryside at home.

FLOURISHING BLOSSOMS

Wreathed in the towering tendrils of a climbing shrub, this small house looks out on a fertile garden in full bloom. Additional flowers are planted in stone troughs stood on old saddle stones.

COTTAGE GARDEN LAYOUT

- *In order to avoid creating a rural jungle, the different sections of a garden need to be knitted together, to have what Lutyens called a backbone.*

- *One way of uniting the whole space is to link each area by a central path; another is to make use of the natural rise or fall of the garden, directing the eye towards a key feature such as an arbor, a garden seat or a favourite view of the countryside.*

- *It helps to use dividers of the same material – beech hedges or low walls built of recycled bricks – and where those dividers reflect local custom, so much the better. Protected by a hat of old roofing tiles, cob or earth walls are best of all since they absorb the midday heat and then release it slowly throughout the night.*

- *Aspect, climate and soil type all play their part in shaping the garden, but a diverse community of fruit, flowers, vegetables and herbs will help to establish a natural ecological balance.*

- *Vegetables can be grown in tightly-packed rows in the beds of organically rich soil. Rotating the crops, or moving them to a different part of the garden each year, avoids a build-up of pests and diseases.*

- *Mixing vegetables and flowers in the cottage garden had a practical application: brassicas such as cabbages and cauliflowers, disguised among the flowers, are less liable to attack from pests.*

- *Different plants suit different climates. However, by creating mini habitats like a chemical-free zone for wild flowers or a damp patch for ferns, a series of separate but interconnecting gardens can be created to give variety.*

- *The woodland copse, constructed from a few low-growing birch and dusted with snowdrop and bluebell blossom; the alpine garden sheltering sedums and stonecrop; the scented garden and the Mediterranean patio garden can all find a corner within the cottage garden.*

PLANTING

Grown for their soaring spikes of flowers which produce a wall of blossom in summer and early autumn, hollyhocks thrive in a well drained soil and full sun. Appropriately associated with country gardens, the hollyhock had already found its way into cottage gardens by the fifteenth century; it was among those listed in a poem penned by John the Gardener in 1440, along with plants like foxgloves, roses, lavender, cowslip and catmint.

Then as now, such flowers flourish in a well-fed and nourished soil. Forked over and cleared of weeds in the winter, flower borders need a rich top dressing of compost or well-rotted manure before the plants begin their spring growth.

In an established garden, plants need to be thinned out and divided to avoid overcrowding. In a new garden, plants bought from the nursery, or passed on by a benevolent neighbour, are planted with an eye on their final height and mass; hollyhocks, which may need to be staked, are best grown against a sunny wall at the back of the flower bed to create a backdrop for intermediate and low growing plants.

STRUCTURES AND DIVIDERS

Ever since people-pressure sent settlers to the far corners of the globe, the cottage gardener has been keen to adopt the best of the plant hunters' finds. The chrysanthemum, which arrived in Holland from China in 1689, was firmly established in small gardens by the nineteenth century, while tulips brought from Constantinople in 1554 became valued collectors' items in the seventeenth century, only to become commonplace in lowland Europe a century later. Tobacco, sunflowers and that monarch of vegetables, the potato, were brought to Europe from the New World and rapidly utilized by the cottage gardener.

Garden features and dividers were also taken from one country to another. Holly, box, yew and other evergreen hedges, pergolas dripping with roses, wisteria-hung trellises, dry stone walls and larch-lap fences all crossed national frontiers as garden fashion demanded.

However, the cottage gardener was less concerned with keeping up appearances than with keeping animals in or out. The cottager who allowed his prize ram to stray from grazing his orchard and sample his neighbour's bean patch could spark off a lifelong feud, and the Danish expression that 'good fences make good neighbours' was, and still is, a prudent code of conduct.

As with the stone or timber of the cottage itself, materials for fencing were gathered from the immediate surroundings. In Provence and the Pennines, stones cleared from the field were built into mellow walls which surrounded the property; in England, blackthorn saplings were planted and laid as stockproof fences – an effective hedge was one that only allowed the wind to pass through it. In North Wales and Brittany, fangs of slate waste were stood on end and wired together to create animal compounds, while in well-wooded districts thin slivers of riven ash or chestnut were turned into fence poles and runners. The thinner brushwood supported the beans and was fixed securely to cottage walls to provide a purchase for Virginia creepers, trailing roses and other climbing plants.

In much of contemporary America and southern Europe, a fence between the house and the road is considered unnecessary, even antisocial, although the natural protection of a stand of fir trees or pollarded poplars is useful to protect fruit trees or vines from unseasonable winds and rain. But where a hedgebank is part of the local landscape, it should be retained and restored wherever possible. A ragged bank of quick thorn, beech and elm which is taken out and replaced by a bare post and rail fence or a regimented line of conifers, does a disservice to both the local landscape as well as the local wildlife.

Although numerous materials are available for today's cottage gardens, from ornamental concrete blocks and galvanized wire structures to plastic framework and netting, the rural landscape still looks at its best when furnished with partitions made from natural materials. The Italian pergola, a sheltered walk which leads to some feature of the garden, and the arbor (which does not) can both be bought-in ready-made from garden centres. Pergolas may be made with treated battens set over a wood or iron frame and arbors from pre-formed wire or iron structures which are gradually cloaked beneath a plait of ivy and clematis. Natural arbors can be grown from a stand of hazel or hornbeam, their tops knitted together and the leafy framework laced with heady-scented climbers such as jasmine and honeysuckle.

ECHOING ARCHES

Two painted arches mirror one another in a tranquil corner of New York State Garden. Combining climbing plants like clematis and roses or honeysuckle and wisteria will give a rich mix of colour and scent.

CONTAINERS

- *Container-grown plants make for a mobile garden: gardeners at the Palace of Versailles kept almost two million planted pots at the ready, changing displays while the Sun King dined. Pot-grown plants can extend the flower power of the smallest garden and turn the most unpromising collection of plants into an Eden.*

- *This otherwise unproductive corner (above) is ornamented with pots and barrels of flowers. Containers have their functional applications too. Pot-grown herbs can be brought inside for use in the kitchen, while an old biscuit tin buried in the herb garden will control invasive plants like mint.*

- *Where a mature tree provides difficult growing conditions at its base, red geraniums stand proudly in terracotta pots (left) to form a circle of colour.*

- *Frost-sensitive flowers like geraniums and begonias can be over-wintered in their containers in a cool conservatory. These ceramic flower pots (above) are taken inside when the weather turns cool.*

- *Pot-grown shrubs (left) set against a cool north-eastern wall for the summer can be placed against a more sheltered southern wall for the winter.*

- *Anything from a formal gilded urn to a pair of old wooden clogs can be used as a plant container. What the plant requires is space to grow, good drainage and regular feeding. Ensure the base of the container has drainage holes and line it with small stones or pieces of broken pot before adding some rich compost and placing the plant inside it.*

CONSERVATORIES

A conservatory is the one structure no one would expect to find as part of a country cottage a century ago. Things are different today.

Many country cottagers have brought a little of the outdoors inside by adding on a conservatory. The conservatory has also found favour as an ecologically-friendly addition to a building, with a heat store in its foundations and a solar heating system in its roof.

Filled with flowering plants and pot-grown shrubs, furnished with wickerwork and protected from the noonday summer sun by white canvas blinds or breezy muslin, the conservatory emulates its grand, Victorian forefathers.

The vogue for the glazed outhouse sprang from the work of people like Decimus Burton who built the Palm House of the Royal Botanical Gardnes at Kew and the gardener Joseph Paxton, responsible for London's Crystal Palace. The Victorians used the same materials – ironwork and glass – and installed oppressive heating systems to sustain the exotic foreign plants which their relatives mailed home from far-flung corners of the Empire.

The French *serre*, a glass extension which could be used as a small sitting room, was less ambitious, and more in keeping with the modern cottage conservatory. Accompanied by a marble-topped café table and a set of metal-framed chairs, the family could sit and enjoy their evening bottle of Bordeaux surrounded by potted plants in lead-lined plant trays which lay in neat, garden-like decorative rows around the windowsill.

However, a conservatory does not suit every cottage. The southern face of a mellow old half-timbered building will not be enhanced by the addition of a great, white whale of glass and wood; the owners would do better to create a sympathetic garden house instead. Another option would be to adapt part of the house as a sun room, replacing a wall at window height with glass set in frames which harmonize with the cottage windows, or discreetly reroofing a single-storey extension with toughened roofing glass.

Conservatory or sun room, the intention is the same – to recreate the feel of *al fresco* life. Brick or quarry tiled floors, which forgive the occasional overflow of water from the shrubs and flowers, good ventilation and a sound system of shading are basic necessities. One solution to the problem of the over-heated conservatory is to plant a vine outside the building and train it inside to spread across the roof. The annual harvest of grapes which hangs ripening over your head is ample compensation for having to sweep out the annual autumnal leaf fall.

The great advantage of the modern conservatory is the added space and flexibility that it gives a home. At the same time as allowing extra light to flow into rooms which are often dark and dingy before being opened out, conservatories can either become a small room in their own right, acting as an eating area or second living room, or act as additional living space when built on to kitchens or dining rooms, for instance. Another example of their versatility is that they can act as garden 'extensions', bringing the outdoors closer when there is little true garden space on the other side of the French windows.

A QUIET PLACE

An interesting combination of herbs and flowers sits happily in a painted wooden étagère *in a comfortable garden room. Wicker furniture and a tall, elegant window, help to create a calm and restful atmosphere in which to read, relax or entertain.*

OUTDOOR ROOMS

- *Life on the terrace or veranda has been an amiable aspect of country living for generations. The sheltered transition from house to garden not only gives the homeowner a sanctuary when it is too hot or cold to sit in the garden, but also provides a haven for tender trees and shrubs.*

- *A southerly aspect is the ideal place to appreciate the outdoor life while enjoying the comforts of home. Here (left above) a timbered trellis supports a living roof of flowering foliage that is planted in the ground outside and trained up the trellis supports. More plants, set in half barrels along the back wall, create a greenhouse look.*

- *The choice of furniture for an outdoor room depends on how exposed the room is. This wicker* chaise longue *(left below) set beneath the glazed wall of a veranda, beside a table of potted geraniums, can be left out all year round. Canvas directors' chairs, folding wooden camp chairs and pressed steel or wrought iron café chairs with cushions are also ideal.*

- *Tiled or flagstone floors and stone walls act as a heat trap, warming up during the day and radiating the heat out in the evening. Vents can be set low down on the house wall to direct some of the heat back into the home at night. Where the veranda is open to the elements (left above) the floor should drain away from the house.*

- *The steps leading up to this open porch in Connecticut (left below) also act as staging for an aromatic display of shrubs and flowers. Confined to their pots these plants need regular feeding and watering. Collect rainwater from the roof in a water barrel to ensure a supply of temperate water for the plants.*

- *There is nothing more relaxing than eating outdoors when the weather permits. Keep to hand a supply of gingham tablecloths and napkins as well as some informal china for easy entertaining.*

AL FRESCO EXISTENCE

A family of red enamel chairs pulled up to an old timber table provides the perfect picture of life in an outdoor room (overleaf). The full-grown tree provides shade and the stone arch frames a doorway into the garden.

REST AND RELAXATION

- *Garden furniture is now available in many different materials and colours. Choose a style which suits your particular type of garden.*

- *Elegantly proportioned wrought-iron chairs and tables fit beautifully into an eating area that is architecturally framed by a clematis- or rose-laden arbor.*

- *Chunky wooden benches treated with weatherproof preservative can sit happily in the garden throughout the year, offering a peaceful retreat from gardening chores.*

- *In a small garden, furnish a seating area with foldaway tables and chairs. Try collecting several wooden chairs, each painted a different colour, for an interesting and variable effect.*

- *If there is space at the bottom of the garden you can create a peaceful haven by training honeysuckle up a simple arbor and placing a wooden seat underneath.*

- *Outdoor entertaining is made easier if you can gather your guests into a defined space. Create an eating area by paving a small space and erecting an awning or by making a change of level at one end of your garden.*

STRUNG OUT

No one can deny that a modest amount of effort reaps its rewards in the garden, but in the heat of the day these tree-hung hammocks (above) invite the gardener to enjoy a well-earned rest.

A PLACE TO REST

The painted table and chair and wrought iron bench (right) are attractive yet functional.

Chapter Six

A COUNTRY HARVEST

The practice of growing what you eat and eating what you grow is as old as the story of the Garden of Eden. The Egyptians filled their pleasure gardens with edible crops such as figs, dates and grapes and, ever since, succeeding generations of gardeners have discovered the delights of feasting on the freshly harvested produce of their own acres.

One for the bowl and one to eat now: few pleasures in life can compare with harvesting the first summer fruit from the strawberry bed.

A little judicious planning and a modest amount of work are all that are needed to coax the least promising garden into being a rich and productive allotment, providing sustenance for a whole family. Fruit, vegetables and animal products are expensive to buy in supermarkets, yet are comparatively easy to cultivate, as long as you have the time, the patience and the space to devote to them.

SHORN SHEEP

In the early summer sun, sheep sheared of their winter fleeces stand in a field of poppies. Grazing animals like these will flourish in the herb-rich sward of a traditional apple orchard.

COUNTRY CROPS

Supermarkets bring food fresh from the field, but by the time it has been transported, washed, graded and packaged, it tastes bland compared to food picked or plucked from the garden and carried direct to the kitchen table. Although our cottage predecessors found much of the necessary work of tilling, sowing, seeding and harvesting the land a time-consuming business, the quality of garden-fresh food was taken for granted by them.

Today those pleasures have been rediscovered and the kitchen garden has once again become a familiar feature. Divided into the traditional four plots by turf, brick or stone paths, crops are rotated around the plots to give their best yield and protect against the build up of disease. In the past the harvest was limited; leeks, cabbage and kale in winter and beans, peas, onion and garlic augmented by the leaves of watercress, dandelion and lamb's lettuce in summer.

Nowadays a succession of brassicas, from cauliflowers to calabrese, follow legumes such as runner beans and peas which, in turn, follow the heavy-feeding potatoes, root crops and onions. Threads of marigolds and parsley grown between crops of carrots help keep away unwelcome insects and brighten the beds, while cloches and cold frames extend the growing season. Salad crops of tomatoes and lettuce, grown amongst the ornamental borders, ensure an extended harvest of fresh food throughout the summer.

In old cottage gardens the herb bed grew alongside such useful flowers as the apothecary's rose (*Rosa gallica*), which retained its scent when used as a pot pourri, and peonies and clove-scented pinks, crushed into scented waters for sprinkling over washed linen and clothing. An additional source of food came from a stand of hazel or cob nuts, a quiet corner devoted to wild berries and from trees such as fig, olive or elder.

Today's gardens can be equally productive and picturesque. Garden centres offer a bewildering choice of varieties and the new gardener should be guided by the same principles which influenced the work on the cottage itself, conserving what grows in the old neighbourhood rather than buying in precious, highly-bred species.

There has been a sad decline in growing cottage varieties of fruit trees. In England where once there were over 6,000 different apples, nine basic varieties now dominate. Old varieties were the rootstock of today's high-yield commercial breeds and famous varieties like the Bramley apple were developed in the kitchen garden. The Bramley was first sown by Mary Brailsford in her North England garden and given the name of the new cottage tenant, a Mr Bramley, when the tree bore fruit. Where an old tree still survives in the cottage garden it should be identified, pruned and, if possible, propagated. It may lack in yield, and a modest yield is sufficient for most households, but it will not lack in taste.

Every cottage has its own micro-climate in which one variety of vegetable will thrive while another will take ill and decline; a little research at the local café or inn should provide some homely advice on favoured varieties and will often result in a useful exchange of neighbourhood-grown seed. It is worth experimenting to find which readily available plants will grow easily in your soil, especially the more luxurious vegetables such as asparagus or squash, expensive to buy but surprisingly simple to cultivate, as long as the soil conditions are suitable.

Maintaining a good soil means maintaining a good compost heap. Situated in a shady corner where nothing else will grow, fed with kitchen waste, enriched with manure and filled out with grass clippings and leafmould, the humus-rich compost heap will do for the soil what no amount of dubious chemicals and expensive artificial fertilizers will achieve in a year of application.

A century ago, the prevailing sentiment of a family sitting down to eat what they had grown and raised for themselves was one of relief. These days it is more one of satisfaction. Apart from enjoying food whose production involved no unnecessary chemical short-cuts (and every gardener should consider growing crops without the use of pesticides and insecticides), there is a righteous pleasure in eating what you have cultivated yourself.

The cottager was kind to his land because he could not afford to be otherwise. Anyone seeking to re-establish a vegetable plot after it has been swamped by *les mauvaises herbes*, as the French so endearingly call the weeds, should make a series of trial diggings until they retrace the old, rich soil. Well treated, it will perform again and again. The cottage grounds should be planned out with as much attention to detail as is put into the house itself. Areas need to be allocated to fruit and flowers, and stockproof fences and weatherproof sheds provided for any animals. Layout will be dictated by the lie of the land, but a common model is to place flowers and lawns in the foreground, vegetables, washing line and the all-essential compost heap in the middle ground and the orchards and animal quarters, separated by a resolute and impenetrable fence, at the back of the grounds.

There is no mystery to growing a good crop of fruit; a well-fed soil and a good dose of sunshine are all anyone needs (opposite).

The right time to lift vegetables and herbs depends upon the season. Here (above) garlic, onions and lavender dry naturally in the sun.

Within this arrangement there is room for a hive of bees, situated so that the flight path does not normally cross the garden path. And where the henhouse is close to the cottage, avoid keeping a cockerel: his summer morning call will anticipate the family alarm clock by several hours.

HERBS

Herbs are among the most perfect plants for a cottage garden. Their versatile culinary, medicinal and scented properties and their ability to be cultivated in poor soil means that they form an important element in the traditionally self-sufficient rural garden. In the past, cottage herbs were grown in beds close to the kitchen door so that they could be used fresh from the soil, for cooking, strewing or soothing. Nowadays, many cottages (and urban apartments for that matter) still have a container filled with herbs near to the kitchen.

Herb gardens have enjoyed a phenomenal revival in recent years as people have once again learnt to appreciate the safe healing properties of herbs. Likewise, a return to natural cooking ingredients has meant a renewed interest in herbs as natural flavourings for the kitchen. Natural scent, too, in the form of pot pourris, has begun to replace the ecologically dangerous aerosol air freshener.

How far you wish to recreate a traditional herb garden depends on available space and what type of garden already exists. It can be as modest as a terracotta pot filled with a few culinary herbs like thyme, parsley and sage or as grand as a symmetrical Elizabethan knot garden, neatly planted with repeating areas of scented and medicinal herbs such as lavender, rosemary, camphor and lemon balm.

A herb is defined as 'a plant useful to man either by its leaf, flower, stem or root' so it is not only the humble varieties of parsley and mint which fall into this category, but also gloriously decorative plants such as roses, geraniums and honeysuckle. Armed with this knowledge, it is relatively easy to create an entire cottage herb garden that is both practical and highly decorative.

Although the ideal position for herbs is a south-facing plot, they will still thrive if they have some sunshine each day in the summer months. Herbs which positively enjoy shady positions include chives, sorrel and angelica. For edging a bed, plant low hedges of spreading herbs such as lavender, rosemary and hyssop. Remember to plant them quite far apart, as they will quickly spread.

Scented herbs provide a delicious aroma both outdoors and inside. Harvest the leaves of roses, bergamot and lilies, and use them to make pot pourris. Alternatively, sew lavender and rosemary into fabric bags to scent clothes and enclose hyssop and rue in small pillowcases to encourage unbroken sleep.

To harvest herbs, pluck them from the plant just before they come into flower. This is the time when they are at their peak condition and giving off their strongest scent.

COTTAGE HERBS

The traditional site for the cottage herb garden should be as close to the house as possible (left below) since the plants are always best used fresh from the patch. The ground beside a new house will not be in good heart and herbs will readily tolerate this relatively poor soil.

Planted among paving stones (left above), herbs like marjoram, thyme, lavender and balm release their scent as people pass.

The young herb bed looks bare and isolated, but remember the plants will rapidly fill out and invade available space. Setting new plants among the flower beds (left below) is one solution; placing them in their own patch, perhaps surrounded by a cartwheel of brick, is another.

HARVESTING AND PRESERVING

The golden rule for harvesting herbs, flowers and produce is the same; pick only the best, while it is at its best. Herbs and flowers should be picked at their peak and dried. Herbs like mint and marjoram, thyme and tarragon can be hung in bunches in a dry, airy shed alongside flowers such as lunaria with their silvery seed pods, yarrow, Chinese-lantern lilies and statice, cut before the flowers fully open. Others, like delphiniums, which keep their colours, can be picked and pressed. Sun, smoke, salt and ice were the traditional means of keeping food fresh and every autumn the cottage kitchen was a hive of activity: beans packed into brine-filled earthenware jars; dried peas placed in mice-proof tins; wire baskets filled with surplus eggs and steeped in buckets of waterglass; root vegetables lifted and stored in earth cellars or straw clamps; onions and garlic dried in the sun and hung in strings; apples cored and dried beside bunches of mint, oregano and lavender. Pots and pans bubbled with jams and chutneys, muslin bags hung from the legs of an upturned stool and dripped pink fruit liquids into china bowls ready for jelly making at the end of the day.

Before the advent of the food freezer, the business of food preservation was a serious cottage craft. Like other country crafts it had almost slipped into oblivion before people realized that the old techniques still have a role to play today.

In the past when the housewife had filled her final earthenware storage jar and placed it with the others on the pantry shelf, she could breath a sigh of relief and begin preparations for that other ancient method of preserving the natural qualities of fruit, the making of wines and ciders for the following season.

The fermenting of alcohol by any other than commercial means is another neglected craft. At one time each country region made its own distinctive brews such as the *eau de vie* of France, Irish *potsheen*, American applejack and the country wines of England. Many traditional recipes were outlawed and lost, only to be replaced by synthetic, sweetened commercial substitutes: a sure measure of the loss is to spend some time with a neighbourly farmer who still keeps a few bottles by for guests.

Although a productive garden in a good year is like an unstoppable flood of food, people today have little time to wholeheartedly follow all the old methods of preserving. The solution is to pursue quality rather than quantity, to stock the freezer with a tray of French beans and peas and to line the pantry shelves with a modest selection of pickled beetroot, shallots, fruit chutneys and relishes. Onions, when sun-dried, can be stored in the legs of old tights, surplus fruit can be pulped and frozen and, mindful of waistlines, low-sugar jams can be made and refrigerated until needed.

HARVESTING HERBS AND FLOWERS

A native of southern Europe, lavender epitomizes perfect country garden produce, not least because it has been neglected over the years (right).

Pick flowers such as poppies (above) as soon as they begin to fade then hang them upside down in a warm place to dry.

KEEPING LIVESTOCK

Many nineteenth-century cottages and most small houses were once little farms grouped around a holding yard, where the cock crowed from the midden heap. Laid out with the site of the pig shed, cow house, barn and byre in mind, these traditional smallholdings were dominated by their livestock, which provided both sustenance and a source of income for the occupiers.

When conditions demanded, the family shared their living space with the animals: orphaned lambs were bottle-fed by the kitchen range and hens roosted in specially built cupboards at the base of the box bed. Occasionally they were judged over-generous. One eighteenth-century writer thought as much when he found himself eating a meal in a North Wales kitchen with 'a large overgrown sow devouring her dinner with considerable dissatisfaction on account of the short allowance'.

Today's generation of cottagers might refrain from keeping such close company with their livestock, but if they can accept the commitment, then the rewards of keeping animals outweigh the effort.

The pig house or sty was once as common as that other familiar feature of cottage gardens, the dovecot or *pigeonnier*. Some stood independent of the house, others were built into a loft or gable end, but both were a sure source of fresh meat in the lean winter months. The goat, the house cow, or the poorman's cow, provided dairy products which, then as now, were easily turned into a range of soft cheeses flavoured with home grown herbs.

These days, a cottage garden is more likely to resound with the calls of a clucking hen or a contented duck rather than a pig or a cow, and there is nothing more satisfying than collecting and cooking eggs from your own hens. Half a dozen good laying chickens will keep a large family in eggs throughout the spring and summer, given fresh water, a handful of grain and room to range about.

ANIMAL MAGIC

Animals are a versatile asset to any self-sufficient cottage economy. They provide food, warmth and company.

INDEX

ACKNOWLEDGMENTS

AUTHOR'S ACKNOWLEDGMENTS

The author is indebted to Joanna Bradshaw, David Laws, Mandy Little, Annik Marsollier, Simon Mole, Jean Perry, Catherine and David Petts, Michelle Seddon-Harvey and Vivienne Southorn.

The publisher thanks the following photographers and organizations for their kind permission to reproduce the photographs in this book:
1 S & O Mathews; *2* Stylograph/Yves Duronsoy/Helene Laforgue; *3* S & O Mathews; *4* Andrew Lawson; *5* Stylograph/Jacques Dirand; *6–7* Reflections Photo Library/Jennie Woodcock; 7 John Heseltine; *8 left* Serge Chirol; *8–9* Jessie Walker; *10* Christian Sarramon; *11* Explorer/M. Smith; *12 above* Explorer/A. Philippon; *12 centre* Paul Ryan/International Interiors; *12 below* Explorer/S. Grandadam; *13* Michael Busselle; *14 above* Ffotograff/Patricia Aithie; *14 below* Explorer/N. Thibaut; *15 above* Serge Chirol; *15 below* Edifice/Hart Davies; *16 above* John Miller; *16 below* S & O Mathews; *17* Michael Busselle; *18–19* Clay Perry; *19* Hamish Parks; *20* Ianthe Ruthven; *21* Edifice/Gillian Darley; *22 left* Michael Busselle; *22 right* Andrew Lawson; *23* Jessie Walker; *24 above* Christian Sarramon; *24 below* Jerry Harpur (Chiffchaffs, Dorset); *25* S & O Mathews; *26 above* Explorer/P. Roy; *26 below* Explorer/F. Jalain; *27 above left* Explorer/S. Cordier; *27 below left* John Miller; *29* Ingalill Snitt; *30 above* John Miller; *30 below left* Explorer/B. Maltaverne; *30 below right* Explorer/P. Roy; *31* Elizabeth Whiting & Associates/David George/Cassell; *32 left* Guy Bouchet; *32 right* Ffotograff/Patricia Aithie; *33* Christian Sarramon; *34* © Image/Dennis Krukowski, 'The Farmhouse', Bantam Books, USA; *35 above left* Elizabeth Whiting & Associates/Jerry Harpur; *35 below left* Jan Baldwin; *35 right* Jessie Walker; *36* Simon McBride; *37 left* Simon McBride; *37 right* Ianthe Ruthven; *38 above left* Agence Top/Pascal Chevallier; *38 above right* Marie Claire Maison/Limbour/Billaud; *38 below left* Pia Tryde; *38 below right* Guy Bouchet; *38–9* © Image/Dennis Krukowski, 'The Farmhouse', Bantam Books, USA; *40* Ianthe Ruthven; *40 below* Amparo Garrido; *41* Paul Ryan/JB Visual Press; *42–3* Peter Woloszynski; *43* Gary Rogers; *44* Daniel & Emmanuelle Minassian; *45* Elle Decoration/Simon Wheeler; *46 above* Tim Beddow; *46 below left* Christine Ternynck; *46 below right* Christian Sarramon; *47* Jeff McNamara; *48 above* Marie Claire Maison/Bailhache/Comte; *48 below left* Antoine Rozes; *48 below centre* Fritz von der Schulenburg (Villa Vicosa); *48 below right* Simon McBride; *49* Kari Haavisto; *50* Elizabeth Whiting & Associates/Tim Street-Porter; *51 above* Elizabeth Whiting & Associates/Spike Powell; *51 below left* Marie Claire Idées/Chabaneix/Chabaneix/Bastit; *51 below centre* Christian Sarramon; *51 below right* Agence Top/Pascal Chevallier (courtesy of Michel Sauboua, Director Epsilen Gallery, Lyon, France); *52* Simon McBride; *53* Explorer/L. Girard; *54–55* Bent Rej; *56* Marie Claire Maison/Bailhache/Comte; *56 below* Gary Rogers; *57* Ianthe Ruthven; *58 left* Karen Bussolini; *58 right* Amparo Garrido; *59* Derry Moore; *60–61* Marie Claire Maison/Chabaneix/Ardouin; *62 left* Ianthe Ruthven; *62 right* Walter Smalling Jnr; *63* Jean-Pierre Godeaut; *64–5* Tim Beddow; *65* Jean-Pierre Godeaut; *67* Simon McBride; *68* Christian Sarramon; *69* Guy Bouchet; *70* Jean-Pierre Godeaut; *71* Tim Beddow; *72* Amparo Garrido; *73 above* Ianthe Ruthven; *73 below left* Marie Claire Maison/Snitt/Rozensztroch; *73 below right* Deidi von Schaewen; *75 above* Simon McBride; *75 below left* Elizabeth Whiting & Associates/Spike Powell; *76 left* Ingalill Snitt; *76 right* Derry Moore; *77* Derry Moore; *78* Stylograph/Jacques Dirand; *79* Elizabeth Whiting & Associates/David George/Cassell; *80–1* World of Interiors/Tim Beddow; *82* Hannu Mannynoksa/JB Visual Press; *83* Boys Syndication/Michael Boys; *85* Elizabeth Whiting & Associates/Anaya; *86* Simon McBride; *87* Walter Smalling Jnr; *88–89* Marie Claire Maison/Snitt/Puech/Rozensztroch; *89* David Phelps; *91* Amparo Garrido; *92 above* Paul Ryan/JB Visual Press; *92 below* Christian Sarramon; *93 above* Antoine Rozes; *93 below* Jean-Pierre Godeaut; *96* Jessie Walker; *96 below left* Lars Hallen/Design Press; *96 below right* Paul Ryan/International Interiors; *97 above* Deidi von Schaewen; *97 below left* Ianthe Ruthven; *97 below right* Stylograph/Jacques Dirand; *98 above* Ianthe Ruthven; *98 below* Arcaid/Richard Bryant; *99* Walter Smalling Jnr; *100 above* Boys Syndication/Michael Boys; *100 below left* John Miller; *100 below right* Houses & Interiors/Simon Butcher; *101* Paul Ryan/JB Visual Press; *102* Jerome Darblay; *103* Paul Ryan/JB Visual Press; *104–105* Simon McBride; *106* Marie Claire Maison/Chabaneix/Chabaneix/Bastit; *107* Deidi von Schaewen; *108–109* House & Interiors/Simon Butcher; *110 left* Simon McBride; *110 right* Houses & Interiors/Ed Buziak; *111 left* Christian Sarramon; *111 right* Houses & Interiors/Simon Butcher; *112–113* Marianne Majerus; *113* Elizabeth Whiting & Associates/Marie O'Hara; *115* Arcaid/Richard Bryant (Mr Baker's garden); *116 above* S & O Mathews; *116 below* Jerry Harpur (Dolwen, Llanrhaedr-ym-Mochnant, Powys); *117 above* Andrew Lawson; *117 below* Gary Rogers; *118–9* S & O Mathews; *121* Jerry Harpur (Designer: Bruce Kelly, New York); *122 left* Amparo Garrido; *122 right* Deidi von Schaewen; *123 left* Marijke Heuff (Mr & Mrs Heymans Christiaans); *123 right* Gary Rogers; *124 above* Amparo Garrido; *124 below* Ingalill Snitt; *125 above* Dia Press; *125 below* Agence Top/Pascal Chevallier; *127* Fritz von der Schulenburg (Robert Kime); *128–129* Agence Top/Pierre Hussenot; *130* Yves Duronsoy; *131* Brigitte Thomas; *132–133* John Miller; *133* Elizabeth Whiting & Associates/Di Lewis; *134* S & O Mathews; *135* Gary Rogers; *136* IMP/Marie-Louise Avery; *137* Andrew Lawson; *138* S & O Mathews; *139* Brigitte Thomas; *140 above* Serge Chirol; *140 centre* Simon McBride; *140 below* S & O Mathews; *141* Christian Sarramon; *142–3* Design Press/Lars Hallen; *144* Agence Top/Pascal Chevallier.